RigVeda MADE EASY

Rigvedic Stories Based on Selected Verses

Sathish Chandra

INDIA · SINGAPORE · MALAYSIA

To my parents, with a deep sense of
gratitude and humility

Contents

Preface

The first mantra of the eighty-ninth hymn of the First Mandala of the Rigveda starts with a great aspiration of the Vedic era. It chants, "Let noble thoughts come to us from every side—unimpeded, unmolested and without any trace of hatred," ("Ano Bhadrah Kratao Yantu Vishwath…"). This one 'Maha Vakhya' (Great Line) from the epic is enough to declare the Rigveda's unique narrative amongst other religious texts. Therefore, this text is all-inclusive and the most secular of all ancient spiritual compositions.

But for laypersons like you and me, who need help understanding Sanskrit, it can be challenging to get to the very essence of the epic. On a cursory glance at the epic, it is no wonder that we get lost in the vast maze of the compositions and its several translations with multiple interpretations. Your confusion worsens, especially when looking into the historical background of this superb composition. Nevertheless, the effort is worth it in the measure of gold.

Similarly, the historical aspects of these compositions are tricky because the epic is very frugal in disclosing the details. After all, the spiritual or liturgical inputs were the focal points for the 'rishis' who composed these poems. What happened during that time was mentioned just as a passing reference. Apart from these features, the text is in archaic Sanskrit and composed in a flowery, poetic language to add to the difficulty for ordinary readers.

Yet, this grand epic of the Indian subcontinent throws enough glimpses into the life, beliefs, culture and civilisation of the bygone era of our country. Historical aspects of the age come as a bonus, nicely packaged with the Vedic God, Indra's bravery and courage. The text also remembers the famous kings with their share of glory.

It is challenging for ordinary readers to get the flavour of the glorious Vedic past without spending many years of focussed readings. When I ventured into the arduous task of studying this excellent text, I was initially frustrated by the repetitive praises of deities of the Suktas. It took years to get the hang of these poems.

It's heartening to note that fundamental ideas of Hinduism are rooted in the Rigveda. The text is one of the oldest and longest collections of poems. Our millennials and young adults want to know what these beautiful poems contain and their significance. Therefore, I have dared to put this simplified and uncluttered version of the Rigveda in an abridged book form. This book contains the gist of what I gathered from my readings to benefit all those who do not have enough time to spare.

This book is created only to give a flavour of the text and the historical background of the Rigveda. I earnestly hope that the book answers many important questions which arise in our minds about the text.

With great humility, I welcome suggestions for improving this text.

Sathish Chandra.

jschandra53@gmail.com

***

Prologue

The Rigveda Samhita is a massive collection of mantras with ten thousand five hundred and fifty-two verses decorating one thousand and twenty-eight hymns of the text. If printed side by side on pages, the book's size may extend to a thousand pages. This core text is quintessentially Indian, which was composed by hundreds of rishis, thus showcasing their poetic talents. Scholars have identified three hundred and sixty-five rishis, including women rishis who contributed to the Samhita. These creative mantras are still a mainstay of Indian religiosity—though they were composed about four thousand to four thousand and five hundred years ago. The Samhita has ten Mandalas or chapters—also called ten Books by many.

Does it contain only philosophy?

When somebody mentions the name 'Rigveda' to us, the first thing that comes to mind is the dry philosophical sermons it may contain. But contrary to the general belief, the text has only a dash of philosophy here and there. More than anything else, the world's most ancient religious text is full of stories—about Indra, the neglected new bride, a rishi going to the chariot race with his young wife driving their cart and a high priest of a 'yajna' talking to a young girl about sex in the open. It contains even the love story of an earthly king and an angel, a bit of advice from a hardcore gambler, the lament of an insecure wife, tips about how to crush your enemy and many other compelling episodes from the yesteryears. It also leaves behind dense historical imprints of the past. But sadly, only a few have ventured to study the Rigveda for its historical input.

Why are laypeople reluctant to read the Rigveda?

Many causes discourage ordinary mortals from reading the text—the first in the list, perhaps is the language in which it is constructed and its poetic nuances. The text is in archaic Sanskrit, and even modern Sanskrit scholars cannot comprehend its true essence. One must depend on various commentaries to grasp the verses that adorn the Rigveda. Another reason why the commoners hesitate to read the text is because of the dire warnings given by the Vedantic scholars. "We have to be careful," they warn, "while chanting the poems from this epic!"

"Remember, any mispronunciations will bring untold miseries to you and your family," they proclaimed.

Sayana, a thirteenth-century Vedic scholar, cautions us that, "The Vedas have hidden secrets. The text is for 'Ninya Vachamsi'—meant only for holy souls," he says.

Another caveat which was usually thrown at us was, "Listen to only trained Sanskrit scholars and their interpretations. They know what to read in the text and what to ignore. Never go by the translations available. They are done by the uninitiated with some ulterior motives."

Unfortunately, the mystical aura created around this enchanting and energetic text successfully turned the gen-next away from reading it.

The most intriguing explanation is that the Rigveda came from the Gods and was revealed directly to the rishis who composed it. Therefore, it contains an aura of mystery attached to the words spoken in the poem. According to Vedic scholars, it is in a coded poetic form and could be grasped by the genuinely knowledgeable— who can decode the profound meanings of what is said. The claims made by the scholars are valid to a certain extent.

It Is a Whole Package

The truth differs from all the warnings and caveats thrown at us. You will be amazed to trace the verses from the Rigveda recited during the 'Havana,' which is performed to celebrate the new arrivals in the family. Some of the mantras chanted during the marriage ceremony of the modern era come from the Rigveda. Even those uttered in front of the funeral pyre of the elders emanate from that sacred scripture. It is a whole package. Vedic people's glittering lives, beliefs, customs, traditions and how they conducted themselves are all recorded there. Nothing is hidden! Everything comes to life in the mantras that are nicely organised and set to different metres in respective hymns or Suktas. The text also contains a treasure of history woven into its narrative.

The Rigveda is the most sacred Indian text—an ancient poetic treatise praising the Gods in heaven. The rishis extensively used these chants during fire rituals of the era. The students also used the scripture during the Vedic period as a 'Complete Knowledge Transfer Guide.' You will agree with me once you go through the book. The practice of writing was not prevalent in that era. Hence, the students were mandated to learn the Vedas thoroughly and made to memorise verbatim all the mantras in the same sequence.

The poets depended on a robust oral tradition in ancient India. The Rigveda is the world's first collection of poems, which give you goosebumps, even today if chanted by trained voices. Its vast content, structure and storytelling methodology attract curious minds worldwide.

Before going further, let us briefly look at all the Rigvedic (RV) Mandalas to know what they contain. Initially, about ten influential families of the Vedic rishis and their associates used to recite various mantras, thus invoking the Gods during their routine fire rituals. Centuries later, these verses grew in number and went out of control—creating confusion amongst the believers. To standardise the usage of mantras, the wise people of the era worked relentlessly to edit the verses and compile them as a compendium.

Though many Samhitas or compendiums came up, only one compiled by Rishi Shakala survived the test of the time. He did a neat job in arranging the mantras in ten Mandalas and discarded repetitive and irrelevant ones.

Mandala (Chapter or Book) One

The first Mandala comprises one hundred and ninety-one hymns or Suktas. The first verse of Hymn One praises Lord Agni, whose name is the first word of the Rigveda. The remaining hymns and poems eulogise Agni, Indra, Varuna, Mitra, the Asvins, the Maruts, the Ushas, Surya, the Rubhus, Rudra, Vayu, Brahaspati, Vishnu, Heaven and the Earth and the Vishvedevas (Universal Gods). This Mandala is not the oldest Mandala of the Rigveda despite being numbered 'One' by its editor, Shakala. On the contrary, it is one of the recent Mandalas. Scholars opine that the mantras of some prominent rishis who did not get an independent Mandala were showcased in this first chapter. It contains two thousand and six mantras or verses.

Mandala Two

Mandala Two contains forty-three hymns and praises, mainly devoted to Agni and Indra. These hymns were composed by Rishi Gṛatsamada Saunahotra and his family and associates. This chapter contains only four hundred twenty-nine mantras—one of the shortest Mandalas. It is a family book for the authors.

Mandala Three

Mandala Three comprises sixty-two hymns, dedicated mainly to Agni, Indra and the Vishvedevas (all Gods literally). Verse 3.62.10 is vital in Hinduism, popularly known as the Gayatri Mantra. Most hymns in this book were composed by the Vishwamitra family. This Mandala is a family book for the Vishwamitras and contains six hundred and seventeen verses.

Mandala Four

Mandala Four's chants praise Agni and Indra and the Rubhus, the Asvins, Brahaspati, Vayu and Ushas. Vamadeva Gautama sang the majority of the hymns in this book. This book is his family Mandala. Fifty-eight poems with five hundred and eighty-nine mantras adorn the text.

Mandala Five

Eighty-seven hymns of this book mainly praise Agni and Indra, the Visvedevas, the Maruts, the twin deities—Mitra-Varuna and the Asvins. Two poems praise Ushas (the Goddess of dawn) and Savitr (the Sun God appearing after the Goddess of the dawn, Ushas). Most hymns in this book were composed by the Atri clan of rishis and belonged to their family. Seven hundred and twenty-seven verses beautify this book.

Mandala Six

Mandala Six comprises seventy-five hymns, mainly praising Agni and Indra, the Vishvedevas, Pusan, the Asvins, Ushas, etc. Most of the hymns in this book were composed by the Brahaspatya or the Bharadvaja family of the Angirasas. This family book of the Angirasas contains seven hundred sixty-five mantras.

Mandala Seven

The poetic wonder of Rigvedic times' seventh Mandala comprises one hundred and four hymns devoted to praising Agni, Indra, the Visvedevas, the Maruts, Mitra-Varuna, the Asvins, Ushas, Indra-Varuna, Varuna, Vayu (the Wind God), two each to Sarasvati (ancient river/Goddess of learning) as well as Vishnu and others. Most hymns in this book were composed by the Vasiṣṭa Maitravaruṇi family and their associates. This Mandala is their family book and contains well-crafted eight hundred forty-one mantras of importance.

Mandala Eight

This mandala comprises one hundred and three hymns to various Gods. The Kaṇva clan of rishis composed hymns 1–48 and 60–66, and the rest were created by the other (Angirasas) poets. Two families share the honour of crafting this Mandala. The number of mantras inhibiting the book is one thousand seven hundred sixteen.

Mandala Nine

This mystic Mandala comprises one hundred and fourteen hymns devoted to Soma Pavamana, a plant's cleansing extract or the Vedic religion's sacred potion. The book contains mysterious details about the potent brew of the Vedic period, Soma. One thousand one hundred eight mantras adorn these hymns.

Mandala Ten

This glorious Mandala comprises one hundred and ninety-one hymns addressed to Agni, Indra and other deities. It contains the Nadistuti Sukta, which is in praise of rivers and is vital for reconstructing the geography of the Vedic people. The Purusha Sukta, which is crucial in Vedic sociology studies and alternative creation stories, is a part of the Mandala.

The tenth Mandala contains the Nasadiya Sukta (10.129), which again deals with multiple speculations about the creation of the universe. The marriage hymns (10.85) and the funeral hymns (10.10–18) from this chapter are still crucial in performing the rituals in the modern era.

This book is undoubtedly the last one to be created by the rishis. The book reflects the shift in the thinking of later rishis from transactional and ceremonial offerings to a more sublime and meditative analysis of religiosity and philosophical aspects. This critical book contains one thousand seven hundred fifty-four mantras.

The Rigveda is a collection of mantras and does not contain any prose. Rishis extensively used these mantras in 'yajna' rituals. The Vedas are called 'Shruthi,' and everything related to the Vedas is called 'Shroutha' (What is heard or revealed).

The Rearranged Version of the Mantras

The verses or mantras were created and chanted by a host of rishis, their family members and associates over a few hundred years. Rishis extensively used them during daily fire rituals. A few rishis had undertaken the systematic arrangement of the verses in the interest of brevity for the learning purposes of future generations. Out of these Samhitas (or the books containing the rearranged mantras), the Shakala Samhita, edited by Rishi Shakala and the Bhashkala Samhita by Rishi Bhashkala, survived the test of time. Again, out of the two, Bhashkala Rishi's volume was elaborate, containing far more details than the Shakala Samhita. Bhashkala's edition could only last briefly against the crisp, sharp edition by Shakala. Bhashkala's compilation of the verses is lost forever. We do not have a copy of that edition. Shakala's Samhita (collection of mantras) won, and we have only his edition for our reference to take a peep into Rigvedic history. It is a significant loss that we do not get to read Bhashkala's books which were supposed to have contained far more essential details.

The problem with Shakala Samhita is that we are yet to know precisely the chronological order of these ten books which he left behind. His collection of verses contains a bare minimum amount of information. Added to that, he has perhaps chosen mantras mainly required for liturgical purposes of the Vedic era. Therefore, the text is full of mantras (about 60%), eulogising the Vedic deities, inviting them to the fire rituals to accept the oblations offered and finally, urging them to shower wealth, health and prosperity on the performers of the ceremonies. These mantras are not beneficial for history buffs as they do not give information about past happenings.

Poetic and Storytelling Skills

However, any serious reader of this text will be amazed to find a cryptic description of the Vedic Gods, and the lavish praises directed at the heavens above give us ideas about people's belief structure. The sheer magnitude of their poetic imagination and how the poems are composed are shining examples of their skills. In contrast, the rest of the world struggled to construct proper sentences in their languages.

More importantly, their storytelling brilliance comes throughout the text. The scripture contains plots and subplots interwoven intricately, which challenges the readers. Yet, we may have to concede it as the Vedic rendering style. The stories come peppered with indicative details suitable to poetic form and do not reveal the complete picture in one place. However, the threads are picked up again somewhere else in the narrative, with a different version or a titbit about the story. More than a hundred such episodes excite you beyond any doubt. This book picks up threads of such stories in one place to make it easy for the readers.

Rigvedic Stories

Though the various hymns tell us past stories in titbits here and there, they also give names of kings, chieftains, rishis and wars which they fought at multiple places. They praise rivers and tell us the order in which they ran in the Vedic region. The geographical markers they discuss in the text, names of tribes the text mentions, the conquests of Bharata Purus, etc., give us many interesting details. Similarly, the Samhita consists of Akhyana or Samvada Suktas (hymns in a dialogue format), providing glimpses into the Vedic thought process.

The Rigveda is a time machine to travel back, discover our ancestors' thoughts and beliefs and know how they led their lives. It is a collection of poems created by people from all walks of life. But unfortunately, commoners believe that it is meant only for the serious types who pursue the spiritual path. Yet, they unknowingly chant mantras from the text while performing their daily poojas at home. Hindu priests unwittingly recite verses from this great book while conducting day-to-day rituals. Many do not even know the origins of these mantras or their meanings.

Why is it so difficult to understand the 'Epic Poem?'

William Shakespeare wrote his highly appreciated plays in early modern English around four hundred years ago. Yet, it is challenging to understand his language for a modern reader. It is difficult for non-native readers to comprehend his tone and tenor. Even native speakers stumble if they read works written in old English. The English language is hardly one thousand and four hundred years old. This aspect holds good with any language spoken in the world today.

Think of Vedic Sanskrit used in the Rigveda, composed somewhere between four thousand to five thousand years ago. The language used there was archaic. To complicate the matter further, we do not have concrete evidence about the background of the people who composed this epic. We have only a hazy picture of Vedic people, their culture, beliefs and the environment. This knowledge comes from the information available in the epic itself. This sacred text is the only evidence to rely upon while trying to decode the mystery hidden in the poems.

On top of all other barriers, the poems by the rishis are filled with figures of speech, as well as a play on words and metaphors of their era. They contain words with elusive and multiple meanings.

The Timeline

Many Western scholars opine that the composition of the Vedas must have begun around fifteen hundred BCE and ended by five hundred BCE. In contrast, some Indian scholars claim that the compendium of the Vedas is as old as eight thousand years. A few Western scholars are trying to link the Aryans and Vedic culture to their famous 'Aryan Invasion Theory.' They earnestly believed that the Aryan race from the European grasslands invaded India, thus leading to the Vedic culture. On the contrary, the Indic scholars want to prove that the Vedic culture is the world's earliest civilisation. But unfortunately, there are few shreds of evidence available for various contentions. Therefore, plenty of questions still need to be answered from either side.

On closer examination, we can easily distinguish the biases of Indic scholars who make exaggerated claims about the Vedas' antiquity. Western scholars are much more methodical, and it is challenging to disprove their theories. In this context, a recent book, Genetics and 'The Aryan Debate: "Early Indians" Tony Joseph's Latest

Assault,' by Shrikant Talageri, is a very bold and well-researched presentation. In his book, while dissecting Tony Joseph's writings, which adopt the theories of Western scholars, Shrikant Talageri reiterates what he has said in his earlier book.

The Evidence from the Other Historical Texts

The book referred to here is Rigveda: A Historical Analysis by Talageri. In this book, he has attempted to tread the path which others have not dared to venture. He has tried to recreate Vedic people's history from the Rigveda's narratives and geographical markers. In this book, Talageri puts forward his arguments with the help of other textual evidence. He quotes The Avesta, —the collection of religious texts of Zoroastrianism and Mitanni documents that are historically dated and verified.

Past historians have dated the Rigveda with the help of Western narratives, which were sometimes speculative. Talageri gives his timeline for the Rigveda's composition with a compelling history chronicle.

According to Talageri, the genesis of the Rigveda must have commenced around three thousand BCE and was completed by two thousand two hundred BCE. His primary argument is that the spoked wheels and horse chariots appear only in the later Mandalas of the Rigveda. They are missing in the earlier Mandalas of epic poems. If we take this timeline, we have a more than four-thousand-year-old language. Even a timeline of three thousand and five hundred years, as given by the Western academicians, is not short by any standard. Therefore, it is difficult to understand the archaic Sanskrit used in the poems in its proper context.

The Context, Beliefs and Environment

To truly understand the Vedas, we must learn more about the Vedic period's background, belief system, environment and social setup. Curiously, whatever we could gather about the conditions prevailing in the period comes directly from the text.

The text is in the form of hymns subdivided into verses in the poetic structure, giving us scant information. Ten important families of 'rishis' or 'high priests' and their descendants composed these hymns. The associates of these rishis have also contributed to the core of the Rigveda from time to time. Because of numerous authors, there were disputes amongst the families of the rishis about who did what. The Rigveda's hymns underwent a rearrangement process to settle disputes between the rishis. That was when the Rigveda split into ten Mandalas, adding some redacted verses between the earlier text.

'Rig' (derived from the root 'rruck') means 'laudatory verses,' and 'Veda' means 'knowledge.' The mantras of the Rigveda were composed by the rishis. The Rigveda has complimentary verses praising many Gods and Goddesses. They are arranged as a group of mantras in Suktas dedicated to a particular deity. 'Sukta' means 'well said.' Likewise, 'Samhita' means well-designed/ well-planned /well-laid out. There is a saying in Sanskrit that those who composed the 'Rrucks' were rishis. They were people with an extraordinary talent for creating mantras spontaneously. Otherwise, these rishis were fully involved in worldly matters. The saying also adds that whichever rishi sang the verses became a 'Devata' (a demi-god). Some Vedantic scholars speculate that Vyasa Maharshi rearranged these Rigvedic verses during the Vedic period.

But the reality is different. We have only Shakala Samhita for reference. Two other Samhitas are wholly lost and unavailable. Shakala edited and rearranged the text available to us now, as the name of the Samhita suggests.

Tape Recorder Version

Western scholars, such as Michael Witzel confirm that the mantras did not change through the ages despite rearranging the verses into ten Mandalas. In his opinion, one thousand and twenty-eight Suktas or hymns containing ten thousand five hundred and fifty-two mantras or verses have contemporary materials, and they can serve as snapshots of the political and cultural situation of the Vedic period. These mantras, he asserts, are faithfully preserved. "These texts are equivalent to inscriptions and a sort of oral history and sometimes an autobiography of the period," he claims.

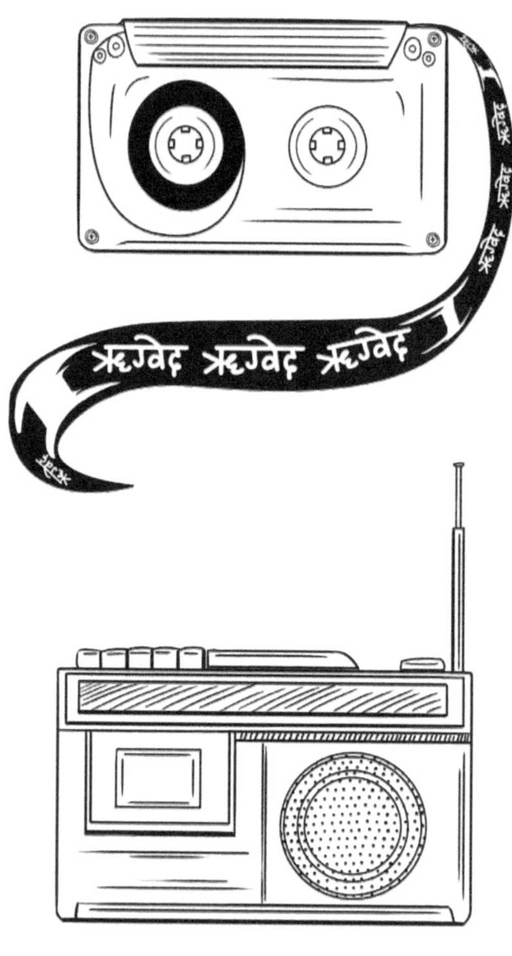

Tape Recorder Version

Further, he adds, "We must regard them as tape recordings made during the Vedic period, transmitted orally and usually without the change of a single word."

Early Translations by the Western Scholars

Here, we must be indebted to the Western scholars for their translations of the Rigveda. Otherwise, it would have been much more difficult for the younger generations to understand the text realistically. Ralph Griffith (1826–1906), an English Indologist, was one of the first Europeans to translate the Rigvedic hymn, and another great scholar, Max Muller, followed by adding the Rigveda to the Sanskrit text. Horace Wilson has written an English text version to accompany Max Muller's copy. Herman Oldenberg has given us the first hypothesis on the chronology of the Rigvedic Mandalas based on comparative linguistic analysis. These scholars have given us realistic text versions and faithfully recorded their unbiased views. I have adopted their translations liberally in this book.

All these scholars have used the extensive help of multiple Vedantic scholars of their era from India for their translations. Sayanacharya, a thirteen-century scholar from the court of the Vijayanagar Empire who wrote commentaries on the Rigveda, was their reference point.

Of course, a few Western scholars had an axe to grind. They wanted to propagate further the hegemony of European rule over India. No doubt, Max Muller did a lot to popularise the study of the Rigveda in Europe. But, he believed that the Steppe Europeans were the first to civilise the barbaric Indian subcontinent. Max Muller has unabashedly claimed that the second coming of the Europeans into the subcontinent was yet another opportunity to discipline and civilise the depraved Indian masses. In a way, he was indirectly suggesting the superiority of Europeans. When the colossus of the Indus Valley civilisation came to light, it gave Western scholars blushes, providing proof of the supremacy of Indian culture over the beleaguered steppe pastoralists who strolled into the continent.

We get an exhilarating feeling when we take a Rigvedic peep into history. It is like picking up cultural superiority points from the hymns and verses that adorn the text. Only the core text of Shakala Samhita is used for reference in this book. Its supplementary texts, such as the Brahmanas, the Aranyakas and the Upanishads, have not been discussed.

As we have seen, the text contains repeated praises of mighty Indra, Agni and other Rigvedic Gods and Goddesses. It will be difficult for us to get to the essence of the sacred book if we get into those verses. Therefore, it will be apt to learn the Rigveda through the stories in the text. We can also understand the Vedic era's history with these episodes' help. It also gives me an advantage as a storyteller. I can pick any verse from any hymn and connect it to the Vedic society to highlight their lifestyle, beliefs, social order, food habits, culture and thinking.

Happy reading.

✳✳✳

1

The Story of the Mighty Indra

Indra is one of the most impressive and prominent deities in the Rigveda. He is associated with many different roles and functions. Indra is the God of thunder, rain and war. He is also a mighty warrior who wields a thunderbolt and rides a chariot driven by heavenly horses.

Indra is also associated with fertility and the abundance of crops, as he is the one who brings rain and fertility to the earth. In addition, the Vedic poets invoked Indra to help them overcome their enemies. Hence, praises for his strength and courage come throughout the text.

In some hymns, Indra is a creator God who brings order to the world and protects the cosmic order ('Dharma'). He is sometimes depicted as a leader of the Gods and is a mediator between the Gods and humans.

Overall, Indra plays a central role in the Rigveda and is one of the most important deities in the Vedic pantheon.

Look at how the Rigveda describes their Commander-in-chief, Indra: "Oh, Indra, you are so beautiful, tall and handsome with a well-shaped chin—you are 'Hiranya Keshi' (one with golden hair)."

In another episode, a woman rishi, Apala, meets Indra on her way. She immediately praises him eloquently and impresses him thoroughly. Pleased, Indra grants her three boons in return for her praises. Without batting an eyelid, clever Apala asks, "Hey, great Indra, you know I have three things which are not yielding anything. Would you please make them fruitful?" (RV 8.80.5–6).

Indra says 'yes' and asks her to name the barren things. "Mighty Indra, my land is not yielding me anything. Please make it fertile."

"Done. Name the second boon," Indra tells her pompously.

Apala innocently asks, "My father's head is bald. Please bless him with hair growth."

Indra grants her second wish and asks her to name the third. Then she urges Indra without shame, "It is my barren womb. Please bless me with children."

You know what? She is not even married. She asks for the fulfilment of two wishes in one combined boon—husband and children in her last boon. Or does it suggest something much naughtier than this? Who can tell us? However, Indra grants her third wish without a fuss. If you listen to these banters, you will be tempted to believe that Indra is a living person. This episode in the Epic is one of such events which is narrated. It has many such stories which entertain us with their simplicity. Such a text can never be boring.

In contrast, even forces of nature, such as various shades of the sun, the moon, water, wind, etc., are also praised eloquently in the scripture. This aspect makes us believe that Indra was revered later because of his heroics and bravery in the battles.

The Adventures of Mighty Indra

The adventures of Indra would be exciting and appropriate to start with when we look into the stories of the Rigveda. Rigvedic poets were sure that Indra was the God of Gods, mightier than all universal forces which could be seen or felt. They believed that there was no match to him in strength, power or ability—to crush enemies. Therefore, they praised him accordingly. "Before him, Heaven and Earth bow, at his breath, the mountains quake." (RV 2.12.13.)

"Through dread of thee, Indra, everything upon the earth trembles—yes, even the immovable regions of the air, Heaven and Earth, the mountains and the forests that are otherwise firm tremble at thy progress," (RV 6.31.2).

For them, Indra was the chief of Heaven and the Earth. He was huge and powerful. Rishis made him their hero of the battle.

They believed that without Indra's blessings, nobody could conquer enemies. With such a strong background, Indra appears in almost all the Suktas of the Rigveda. The verses are complete with varied and exciting stories of his bravery, vanity, love for good food, women and the top-class liquor of their era—'Soma.'

During the early evolution of the Rigveda, the lord of the middle realm, or 'Antariksha,' was Indra. It was his battleground because the air above the earth was the home and gathering place for all demons in the form of clouds. Yaska, the earliest commentator of the Rigveda, stated, "There are three Gods, Surya in the sky ('Akasha'), Indra or Vayu in the air and Agni upon the earth."

He also named other Gods of those regions in his writings on the script.

We could see the close association between Indra and Vayu or the Maruts, the wind and storm Gods, in umpteen hymns of the sacred book. But Indra always led them and was at the forefront of all battles in the Suktas. They were an inseparable trio, crucial in all skirmishes, big or small, in the Vedic times.

Indra and His Origins

Yaska, a Sanskrit grammarian and linguist, who commented on the Rigveda about two thousand five hundred years ago, gives us about thirteen different meanings quoting the root of the word, 'Indra.' After studying the commentaries, Western scholars have assigned the meaning of "the stormer or the oppressor (of the enemy)" to the name, Indra which perfectly suits the tone and tenor of the sacred book.

The Vedic poets narrated the birth of this mighty God of the rishis differently. But they were guarded and elusive while giving the names of Indra's parents. Many rishis, in their poems, while eulogising Indra, have given only a passing reference to his parentage. Only in a few verses with the pointed mentions, do they occur.

The Vedic scholars named Aditi as Indra's mother. However, they rarely discuss his father's name because the Rigveda throws different narratives on these aspects.

What does the Rigveda say about Indra's origin?

The seventeenth hymn of Book Number Four details the birth of Indra. It exclaims, "At the time of Indra's birth, Heaven trembled, the earth shook, mountains were agitated, water gushed and deserts flooded" to emphasise the fury of his 'Vajra' (thunderbolt) unleashed by the swift-moving Indra with the howling storms. Though Verse number Four chants, "Thy father, Dyaus," there is no mention of his mother. In the same breath, the poet, in Verse Twelve informs, "Indra does not care either about his father or his mother when furious."

This verse is interpreted as "Indra mercilessly drags Heaven and Earth in whose embrace he was born." Another verse (number Four) of hymn number Twenty-two explains thus, "Mountains and hillsides, the heaven and the earth trembled before the gigantic one (Indra) at his birth. When the brave one brings his parents to the thundercloud, the storms bellow circularly."

There are many such references to the approaching storms, thunder and heavy rains at the time of Indra's birth throughout the ten Mandalas (also called Books) of the Rigveda. Therefore, many scholars believe that

Dyaus (or Akasha/Sky God) is the father and Prithvi (or the earth) is the mother of the hugely built mythological Indra of the scripture.

The Second Version

The alternative birth story of Indra appears in Hymn Eighteen of Book Number Four, which has a human side to it. But the rishis believe that the conception of the mighty God must be nothing short of a miracle. Thirteen verses of this hymn are challenging to decipher because of the multiple stories embedded into it. After a detailed study by many experts, E. D. Perry, a Western scholar, tries to present its gist valiantly. Like him, many have given their versions of this hymn according to their understanding.

The hymn describes how Indra's mother had suffered a lot due to starvation while she was pregnant. The terrible demons had conquered Heaven and had imprisoned all the clouds bearing water in Heaven. None of the Gods could release them from the demons. Indra's mother laments about her abandoned state. It was 'Shyena,' the falcon, (later known as Vishnuvahana Garuda) who had given her the hundredfold strong Soma juice when she was hungry. Indra had absorbed this powerful Soma's essence in the womb and grew into a strong foetus. This background explains why Indra was so fond of Soma.

Indra, yet to be born, had stayed in the womb for a thousand months because his mother hid him. She feared the enemy who killed her husband. "Sahasra maaso jabhaara sharadascha poorvihi" (RV 4.18.3, 'Sahasra masa'—meaning one thousand months, which can also refer to a longer duration).

When Indra's patience ran out, he was too huge to come out in the usual human way. He decided not to be born in the usual painful way, which would endanger his mother. Instead, he wanted to come forth from the womb by bursting open her side—thus creating a unique way for himself—"Tirashchata parshvan nirghamaani" —(RV 4.18.1.) According to the poet, this is uttered by the to-be-born Indra before coming out of his mother's side.

"He sprang up himself, assumed his vesture and filled the earth and Heaven as soon as he was born." (Griffith), (RV 4.18.4 and 5).

When he came out of his mother's womb magically, he was so huge that he took up his battle gear and Vajra, and thundered, "Tell me, who is the killer of my father? In which way I will find him?"

The stunning narrative does not stop there. When the life-supporting womb fluid gushes out, after the birth (may be a metaphoric expression of the copious rain he brings with his arrival), the author, Rishi Vamadeva compares this continuous flow to a river (Kusava) which almost drowned Indra in the womb. Indra holds Vajra with a hundred bolts, specially designed by the celestial designer, Tvastar for him in the womb. Tvastar was also responsible for the perfect shape of the baby in the womb despite the baby's hardships.

The Rigveda 3.32.8 chants: "Yajjaato apiboha Somam."

"Indra became immensely powerful and massive as he drank Soma (the elixir of the Vedic era) soon after his birth," the verse exclaims.

Indra's mother, greatly impressed by his fury, tells him: "The warrior who seeks your enmity is roaring on hills."

Vyamsha, the demon, who had killed Indra's father (he who had won the zone of Heaven), wanted to kill the child and struck him violently. Unperturbed by the attack, Indra smashed the demon's head with his thunderbolt. Indra's mother lovingly calls him 'Maghavan' (the mighty one) as he crushed the monster, Vyamsha who had beaten and killed her husband.

The Rigveda (1.80.6–12) describes Indra's bravery in a war against the hostile powers of the middle realm (Anthariksha) and how he crushed Vritra, the hoarder of clouds.

"With hundred jointed thunderbolts, Indra rushed to the trembling foe, Vritra, struck him on his back, and released the waters to run."

The Rigveda (1.10.9) chants:

"Win us the waters of the sky. And send us kine (hordes of cows) abundantly."

These verses hint at the drought in that period and how Indra killed Vritra, who encircled the clouds and helped people by releasing copious rains to the region. This episode of killing Vritra comes out brilliantly in all praises of Indra while invoking his blessings.

"Tvam deveshu prathmam avamahe" (RV 1.102.9-10).

"We invoke Thee, first amongst deities. You are a mighty conqueror. You won always but You never held back the booty You collected in these battles," the poet chants, expressing the gratitude of the people who benefitted from Indra's largesse. Indra distributed the cattle which he won after killing the demon, Vritra.

In the above narratives, the birth of the hero of the Rigveda is a mix and match between something human and a miracle. At the same time, the first description was purely supernatural. The Anukramani (appendix) of the Rigveda records hymn eighteen of Book Four as the dialogue between the poet Vamadeva, Indra and his mother, Aditi.

Alternate Versions

In many of the verses, there are mentions of Indra's parents but in a very general way without disclosing their names:

"Many thousands do I cast to earth at once, for my father created me as an Irresistible One" (RV 10.28.6).

"A giant begat the giant for battle, a heroine bore the hero," (RV 7.20.5).

"When Thou, Oh, Indra, like the dawn, didst fill both worlds, a divine mother had borne Thee, the great ruler of great nations, a noble mother," (RV 10.134.1).

"While yet an immature boy, He mounted the new wagon and roasted for father and mother a fierce bull," (RV 8.58.15).

Finally, the most puzzling one—"Now at the Soma feast, I proclaim Your heroic deeds. Your parents are slain, overpowered by the Gods. But Ye, Indra and Agni, remain alive."

"He is the son of truth," "He sprang from Horse (the Sun)," "Son of might/strength," "Son of a cow winner," "Indra with Agni sprang from Purusa's mouth," "Indra is the son of Nistigri," "Son of Vrasana" (horse or bull depending your interpretation), are some examples how the Vedic poets addressed Indra. Rishis used these praises to impress Indra and make him come to their fire ritual to grant them their wishes.

Mighty but Fun-loving Indra

The Vedic poets never shied away from humorously portraying the huge, violent and ferocious Indra. He is an antihero in a few hymns. His legendary love for Soma and infatuation with beautiful women have also been discussed elaborately in the mantras. Some classic examples are:

Indrani Sukta

Indra had many wives and was fond of beautiful women. Similarly, the womenfolk would easily fall for him as he was virile, brave and handsome.

Hymn number one hundred and forty-five of the Tenth Mandala is unique in that sense, and it talks about the most potent plant dug out by Indrani, Indra's queen. The hymn tells us how envious she is of the other wives of Indra. With the help of the herb or the plant, she oozes with confidence that she will win Indra back only for herself. And she viciously declares that the herb can destroy the rival wives if it is kept under their pillows. She is confident that the plant will bring Indra back to her like a cow returning to her calf with the speed of flowing water.

She does not stop there and proclaims, "I am the flag," (Aham Ketu). In its essence, she is declaring that the house belongs to her. "I am the head of the family," (Aham Murdah) and "My speech is violent," (Aham Ugrah Vivachini). These proclamations challenge the supremacy of Indra in his house. But when it comes to her son and daughter, she becomes very motherly. Her son is the bravest soldier globally, and her daughter is the greatest without any parallel. The Rigveda includes these mantras, which is extraordinary because Indra's wife challenges their super God's supremacy here.

Are you surprised by the viciousness of Indra's wife? Yes, she was like any other modern wife with her insecurities. The envious wife's utterings make us think that Indra was like any other Chieftain of the Vedic era with polygamous tendencies. The only difference was that he had a knack for winning battles. His aggression and strength come from the potent Soma drink he consumes in copious quantities.

But Indra, too, had his moments of self-doubts. If you do not believe it, read the following two stories.

Heavenly Damsel and King Pururavas (RV 10.95)

The eighteen mantras or verses of hymn number Ninety-five in Book number Ten tell a story of Pururavas's love and Indra's deceit. The story's background is that

Urvashi, the daughter of Ushas (the Goddess of dawn), was beautiful and attractive. Indra was possessive of her and was waiting for an opportunity to bring her to his palace. Some claim that she was already under his spell. But somehow, King Pururavas charmed Urvashi and brought her to his palace.

Being the son of Ila, Pururavas had a reputation as one of the bravest warriors. Urvashi knew about Indra's infatuation with her and therefore put certain quirky conditions before walking into the hands of Pururavas. Her caveat was to save herself from Indra's wrath in case of a showdown between the two men. This incident devastated Indra, and he was looking for an opportunity. One day, finally, he lost his patience and tricked Pururavas into breaking his marriage covenant. Promptly, Urvashi left the king. This hymn depicts a dialogue between Pururavas and Urvashi in which he pleads to her to change her mind. It is so dramatic and colourful that it encouraged many later Sanskrit poets to develop their story versions of the hymn. Let us look at the simplified version of Professor Wilson's narrative.

Pururavas: "Ho, the aggrieved wife, let's sit down and talk. I want to tell you so many things I have not shared."

Urvashi: "The talk is not going to change anything. I have left you like the first of the dawn (when the sun rises). You can't catch me again because I am like the wind. Go back to your palace, Pururavas!"

Pururavas: "I am no more a reckless warrior. I am no more a plunderer of cattle (of enemies). I have lost my prowess and strength. My enemies and valiant warriors do not hear my shouts of command on the battlefield. (I have sacrificed these things for you)."

Urvashi: "I cared for your father, your family and its honour. I loved you whenever you embraced me—day or night. You hugged me thrice a day and loved me without any parallel. I followed you to your palace. You have been my hero."

Pururavas: "The maids like Sujurni and others were always eager to decorate, protect and serve you."

Urvashi: "When you were born, all the wives(of Gods) surrounded you. Flowing rivers nourished thee, and Gods reared you for a mighty conflict and the slaughter of Dasyus."

Pururavas: "They became my companions when you came to me, abandoning heavenly attire. Few fled like a timid doe on seeing me."

Urvashi: "You have been born to protect the earth. Now, the son has taken birth. Knowing (the future), I instructed you (on what to do). You did not listen to me. Now, why do you ask me?"

Look at the melodrama.

Pururavas: "When shall a son (born of you) claim me as a father? Which son will sever the husband and wife who are of one mind? Will he mourn when the funeral pyre of elders is burning?"

Urvashi: "Let me vouch that he will shed tears and cry aloud when the auspicious time comes. I will send that son who is yours in me. Now, go back to your home. You can't retain me, you simpleton!"

Dialogue between Urvashi and King Pururavas

Pururavas: "He (your husband) will go to a far-off land, never to return—either to sleep on the bosom of destruction or to be eaten by swift-moving wolves."

Urvashi: "Do not fall or die, Pururavas. Do not let the wolves devour you. Female friendship does not exist—their hearts are like Jackal's hearts. When I changed in form, I wandered amongst mortals and spent four delightful years. I ate only a small portion of butter daily. Satisfied with that, now I depart."

Pururavas: "I, Vasista, bring you under my command. Oh, Urvashi, who fills the sky (with glory) and measures out the rain—may the bestower of the (fire) ritual (Pururavas) abide by thee. Come back—my heart is burning."

Urvashi: "Oh, son of Ila, you are subject to death. Let your progeny propitiate gods with oblations. You shall rejoice with me (in heaven)."

One Story, Many Versions

Thus, this hymn ends as abruptly as it begins. It does not give us the complete story. The heroes of the Rigveda were the Purus. The protagonist of the hymn is an ancestor of the Purus, as it shows up in his name. Puru clan members must have consisted of a small number in that era. Therefore, everyone in the group knew the story's background and ending. Hence, they gave only a short version of the episode as the composition was poetic. Nevertheless, it is a cute love story.

Unfortunately, the Vedic people focussed on keeping the mantras in their memory as there was no writing.

Thus the people forgot the complete background story. Centuries later, they might have recreated the myth afresh in the 'Puranas' when they realised their lapse. Therefore, different versions emerged over the years.

Rights and Responsibilities

The dialogue throws light on the rights and duties of the husband and wife of that period. The king's foremost responsibility is to protect his kingdom, not chase women. The woman's heart is cunning. So if you go after them, they will ruin you. The husband has his right over the unborn son. Frustrated by Urvashi's refusal to return, Pururavas threatens to commit suicide. But the bold lady did not flinch. And even after invoking the name of Vasista, the powerful rishi of the era, the women dared to refuse co-habitation. Urvashi does not budge even when Pururavas invokes the fire God. These verses point toward the freedom enjoyed by the womenfolk of the Vedic period. You also noticed the dialogue between the couple might match with the present-day husband and wife seeking a divorce.

Returning to our hero, Indra, you can see his cunningness from the above episode. He did not fight Pururavas. Because he must have been equal to Indra in his fighting skills. On the contrary, the hymn's author may be trying to establish that their ancestor, Pururavas was equivalent to Indra.

In the end, Indra cunningly plans Urvashi's departure from the side of Pururavas. This act makes him a mortal like any other scheming king.

The Slaying of Vritra, the Great Serpent

In the Rigveda, the story of the slaying of Vritra repeatedly comes when the rishis decide to praise Indra. 'Vritra' means 'to encircle.' Rishis tell us that Vritra was encircling the clouds. Indra is a thunder God, and he destroys Vritra with his weapon, the 'Vajra' (thunder). When the blocked clouds are released, rain comes in. Because of this story and several others related to natural phenomena, Westerners called the Rigveda a nature myth.

Indra Killing Vritra

Interestingly, Zeus (the thunder God) kills the great serpent, Typhoeus in Greek mythology. But the nature myth is missing there. In Deutronic or Germanic mythology, Thor is the thunder God and he destroys the great serpent, Midgard. In Mittani mythology, the God, 'Inara' (Indra?) kills the great snake.

In Iranian mythology, Indra is a demon. But the slaying of Vritra is remembered there, and Indra is referred to as 'Vitra Harna' (slayer of Vritra). Later stories discussed Vitra Harna as the killer of enemies and revered him.

In their stories, he also removes the obstacles that prevent rain!

In the Mahabharata, the Vritra becomes a Brahmin, and a new story emerges. Indra kills the Brahmin and, as a curse, becomes a leper. He goes into hiding out of shame. Devas anointed Nahusha (the human king) as their head, out of desperation. Of course, this story does not have any connection to the Rigveda. They picked names from the text and told a new account in the Puranic days. The Rigveda gives little information about the terms and expressions in its mantras.

Indra's Messenger (RV 10.108)

There is only a passing reference to Indra bringing back sunlight trapped by the Panis after giving them a hundred blows in Mandala Six (20.4) and Seven (9.2). But hymn number one hundred and eight in Mandala Ten gives us more details. The eleven verses in the Mandala are in the form of a dialogue between the Panis and Sarama.

The storyline is like this—When Indra discovers a herd of cows is missing from his shed, he asks Sarama to find the cattle. Sarama was India's dog messenger and dogs are good at tracing things because of their acute sense of smell. Or is it a metaphor for a woman messenger with good tracking abilities? We do not know.

The Dramatic Dialogue

Sarama finds the cows hidden by the Panis in a cave across Rasa, a mystical river. She goes to the Panis and, in the name of Indra, demands the release of the cows hidden in the cave. The Panis tauntingly ask Sarama: "Tell us, who is this Indra? Let him approach us. We will make friends with him. We can even make him the lord of our cattle head!"

Like a skilled messenger, Sarama tells them, "Nobody can subdue Indra. He can easily cross the mighty river, Rasa and slay you all. He is so powerful. Therefore, I am here to represent him."

The Panis refuse to give in and tell Sarama that they are ready to fight with their sharp weapons and try to seduce Sarama with a bribe offer. "Sarama, you have come from far. Be our sister and stay with us. We will share our cattle with you."

By now, the exasperated messenger of Indra retorts firmly. "I do not recognise any brotherhood or sisterhood. I urge upon you to depart to a far-off place before Indra comes in with the blessings of rishis like Brahaspati and auspicious Soma along with the grinding stones that they found."

With Sarama's warning to the Panis of dire consequences, the hymn ends. Later, sources show that Indra successfully got rid of the Panis in the ensuing battle.

The Trust Deficit

In one of the later versions of the story, Sarama becomes a traitor and does not give Indra any information. When Indra angrily kicks her in the stomach, Sarama throws out the milk given to her as a bribe. Frightened, Sarama runs back to the Panis, trembling in fear. In another version, Indra sends the eagle from heaven to track the cows at first. When he cheats, the Gods strangle Superna, the bird. He omits curds given by the Panis. As a second representative, the Gods send Sarama, a faithful dog.

The Stories Are Copies

It is fascinating to note that, like the 'flood story,' the episode of Sarama appears in Greek and Teutonic (Germanic) myths with some variations. Likewise, the different versions of the heroes killing a mythical giant snake appear in many civilisations worldwide. Ancient Egyptian history shows a hound guarding the underworld alongside their Jackal-headed God, Anubis. Similarly, Indian mythology describes four-eyed hounds guarding the underworld of Yama.

These two hounds of Yama are the sons of Sarama, who appears in our story. Therefore, it is clear that the ancient world had a robust network of communication between them. It is optional to know who copied whom. The stories are retold in every community in the past with variations.

What are the modern interpretations?

The Vedic scholars believe that the Panis were demons, and they used to trap the clouds in the caves to block the rainwater that helped irrigate crops. Others say that day and night, a natural phenomenon, had mystified primitive human beings. Hence, they claim that it is a story about the forces of darkness stealing away the sun or its rays. The vital energies of goodness rescue the sun's rays without any respite regularly from the evil forces. The ancient Egyptians also believed somebody stole the light in the evening and had to be routinely retrieved.

However, according to a more realistic version, the character of hiding away the wealth belongs to greedy traders and merchants from time immemorial. Hence, some claim that the Panis refer to wealthy business people who stored wealth stealthily. Therefore, the word, 'Pani' later developed into commercial terms, such as 'Pana' (money), 'Vani' (trading community) or 'Vanijya' (commercial), etc. You can choose your story version depending on your likes and dislikes. But one thing is sure from the episode— the spies of the kings and overlords of the past played the double game like any other modern spies. They also knew how to intimidate the enemy psychologically before attacking them.

Kosambi's Take

Historian D. D. Kosambi argued that this story is about how the Aryans demanded tributes from the local overlords by harassing them. These assertions make Indra very much a mortal than the 'King of Heaven.' Surprisingly, this alpha-male superhero of the Rigveda fades away after the Vedic period. He also gets involved in extra-marital affairs, thus spoiling many happy families of the Rigvedic era. After the Vedic period, new Gods, such as Shiva and Vishnu became more potent, and the concept of the ultimate reality or Brahman (monotheism) emerged.

Is Indra a tribal head of the immigrants?

Indra would consume Soma eloquently, become like a fully rounded moon and be ready to fight and kill the host's enemies. Indra would become angrier and more ferocious with every draught of the drink that he consumed. With his strength and courage multiplied, Indra would fight for anybody who praised him and offered vigorous oblations. He fights for the Purus and non-Purus in different locations in the text. This kind of description fits well with modern-day mercenaries who have no interest in anything other than enjoying life to the fullest extent. Generally, they come from a distant location. In the first story, Apala praises him as a man with 'golden hair.'

With this description in mind, is it fair to assume that Indra was the tribal head of the Steppe people? Was he eager to fight like medieval Europeans at the drop of a hat if given plenty of food and drink with eloquent tributes? Going further with this thought, curiously, the Rigveda does not refer to him as 'Arya.' According to the text, the Aryas were the Puru and the Bharata clan members, and all others were Dasas or Dasyus.

The text refers to Indra both in the present and past tense. In addition, the scripture records his presence over a long period in many Mandalas. These characteristics make Indra a natural person with a fearless attitude. It is also possible that the tribal head of a particular group was called Indra like the entire progeny of the Angirasas and the Vasistas and other rishis were referred to by the same family name.

Indra Runs Away

In another episode, Indra caught and killed a Dasyu, called Shambara, after chasing him for forty years. It was not a cakewalk for him. In one of the earlier battles with Shambara, when surrounded by the enemy from all sides, Indra gave up his elaborate battle wear to his bodyguard and ran away. The duplicate of Indra, when caught by the Dasyu enemies, declared, "I am not Indra. The one who separated day and night, heaven and earth and killed many demons, that mighty Indra is invincible."

Such is the truthfulness of the Rigveda, which does not shy away from telling the truth. Even Indra had to run away from the battlefield when He was cornered.

Indra as a Drunkard—Laba Sukta (RV 10.119) tells a story about a fully drunk Indra saying, "I do not know what to do. Look at this, I am holding the earth in my mighty hands. I don't know where to keep it. Shall I keep it here? Or there?" Funnily, all the thirteen mantras of this 'Sukta' end with a blatant exclamation of a habitual drunkard. Indra asks, "Did I drink too much of Soma?" ("Kuvit somasyapam iti!")

These verses contain boastings by a thoroughly inebriated Indra.

The hymns of all the chapters of the RV generally begin with an elaborate praise of Indra, Agni or other deities (a God or a Goddess). In these praises, the author, a rishi of the particular hymn repeats the mythological stories of that era, such as the slaying of Vritra or the killing of an enemy chieftain in his typical style. Therefore, we can see similar-sounding verses throughout the Rigveda.

Therefore, the verses and hymns in the Rigveda become monotonous and repetitive. Hence, I have freely moved within the various Mandalas to make the narrative enjoyable.

Why are the narratives so different?

The hallmark of the sacred book was to remain silent halfway when in doubt. The poetic format adopted by the rishis is apt for efficiently keeping the narrative about the unknown or unknowable.

In addition, the mantras appearing in the Rigveda are much older than the compendium which was ultimately compiled by Rishi Shakala around fifteen hundred BCE. These verses were created by different rishis of the early Vedic period using their creative thought process in different periods. Therefore, the narrative about Indra's origin and birth differs vastly, depending upon which family of rishis and the period to which each belonged. For some scholars, various explanations seem confusing and point to the lack of clarity in the minds of the wise people of that era. But the truth is entirely the opposite.

The inclusion of varied stories about the mighty God, Indra in the compendium exhibits the higher tolerance level of the rishis to the conflicting ideas of the Universal Truth. They never insisted or fought with each other about a particular thought. Instead, they accommodated alternative narratives with an openness which was rarely seen in the monotheistic religions of the Western world.

Indra's birth story commences from the nature myth—he is an offspring of natural forces, such as the earth and heaven, sky or Purusha etc. This earliest narrative was in tune with the understanding and belief system of the people around three thousand BCE to five thousand BCE. World over, the Sky God and Mother Earth were treated as the parents of a Godly persona who ruled the world. The Super God of the Vedic era resonates well with this kind of thinking. Therefore, a few believe that the earliest mantras adopted in the Rigveda belong to around three thousand BCE. In a way, the verses in the sacred book prove the antiquity of Vedic thought.

The rishis of the Vedic era were always eager to explore the Ultimate Truth and therefore came out with different ideas and narratives. In the last chapter of the Rigveda, they come out openly with many brilliant takes about the Ultimate Truth and creation stories which would have been blasphemous in monotheistic religions. Even the mighty Indra slowly faded away from importance at the end of the Vedic period.

2

The Stories of Agni and Other Deities

The number of hymns dedicated to Agni in the Rigveda comes only next to Indra. The Rigveda considers fire as the local representative of the Gods on the earth because Lord Agni has a three-in-one status in the Rigveda. In the Akasha (sky), he is the representative of the sun. In the Antariksha (atmosphere), he takes the form of thunder. On earth, he is Agni (fire God). He is also considered the local medium through which people send the oblations to the Gods residing above.

The Rigveda states, "The Bhrigus established Thee, Agni amongst mankind for men, like a treasure—beauteous ease to invoke. Thee, Agni, as a herald and choice-worthy guest, as an auspicious friend to the celestial race" (RV 1.58.6—Ralph Griffith).

Fire and Civilisation

Fire played a critical role in the evolution of human beings in their upward movement on the hierarchical ladder of the animal kingdom. The ancient people must have watched the fire with sheer amazement. Fire appeared on the earth when thunder and lightning struck nearby trees. They must have earnestly believed that fire came from heaven above. Therefore, when they thought of the deification of higher powers, the first thing that must have come to their minds was the fire God because fire gave them everything. Fire gave the people heat in the cold, light in the dead of the night, saved them from the wild animals and helped them to cook their raw food. Also, more importantly, the 'Agni' (fire) always danced upwards and disappeared into the sky in the form of smoke. These characteristics made the ancient people believe that fire always returns to heaven and meets the Gods.

Over centuries, slowly and steadily, a new belief system must have emerged. The fire God became the central deity and mediator between the humans and other Gods and Goddesses in heaven above.

As fire played an essential role in the lives of the people, they started preserving the fire in their respective houses, and thus, they avoided the difficulty of lighting fire repeatedly in those days.

The ninth and the last mantra of the first hymn of the first Mandala pleads to Agni— "Hey, Agni, be unto us easy for our access as is a father to his son. Be ever-present with us for our good."

Lighting fire from "Arani" (the wooden churning pots to create a small fire) was a tedious job, requiring a particular skill. They found the easy way out by preserving the fire in their huts. It was natural for them to restrict the fire within a small area to protect their houses.

When the ancient people noticed that the fire brightened when they poured tiny quantities of 'Ajya' (Ghee) into the mounds, the first joyful utterances must have escaped from one of the poetically inclined rishis. "Oh, Agni, you are so beautiful and amazing! You must have come from a faraway place (Heaven). Here, take some more Ajya. Why don't you give me some rewards in return for these offerings?" These initial verses must have taken shape hundreds of years before the mantras were ultimately collected and compiled as Rigveda Samhita by Rishi Shakala.

The people knew that fire appeared on the earth through lightning and thunder from heaven above. Thus, the fire ritual must have begun, later developing into a formal 'Agni Hotra' or 'Yajna.' When simple fire worship, 'Agni Hotra,' got institutionalised in society, people started offering everything that they relished and ate. They offered 'Charu' (rice), Purodasha (a kind of bread), meat and ultimately Soma (an intoxicant drink that the Purus loved) to the sacred fire. The last mantra of the first hymn of the first Mandala teases Agni with the following:

"Oh, Agni, take these oblations and bring me some gifts as a father would bring them for his sons when he comes back home."

A few things never change—fathers always bring something or the other for their kids when they return home—even today.

The Origins of Agni

"He is the son of Surya (Sun God)," claims the RV 10.73. However, it throws a caveat— "Only Indra knows about Agni's birth."

Lord Agni springs from the mouth of the Universal Being in the Purusha Sukta along with the mighty Indra.

But the RV 6.59.2 proclaims that Indra and Agni were twin brothers emanating from the same father and mother and being everywhere.

Mantras in the text thus give us a variety of versions of the mythological Gods—robustly and beautifully. Different rishis of that era never shirked away from describing Gods in their own way. The other scholars of the age accepted these mantras and interpretations sportingly without making an issue. We, too, must buy these versions wholeheartedly without trying to attribute special meanings to them. That is why I have adopted the straightforward meanings of the mantras. Thousands of writings are available for those inclined to imbibe deeper or metaphysical meanings of these verses.

Fire ritual (Rishis Performing Yajna)

The First Mantra of the Rigveda

The very first mantra of the Rigveda invokes Agni. The first English translation of the epic was by Professor Horace H. Wilson in 1850. Wilson consulted many Vedic scholars of India and followed the famous Sayanacharya's interpretations. He translates the first mantra as follows:

> "I glorify Agni, the high priest of sacrifice, the divine, the ministrant, who presents the oblation (to the Gods) and is the possessor of great wealth."

All the nine mantras or verses of Sukta Number One (or hymn) praise the fire God, Agni. It is evident from the readings of the epic poems that Vedic people believed in various nature Gods. They firmly asserted that the fire God, Agni is the local representative of all the Gods in heaven. Therefore, they offered the oblations to the fire God first and then to the other Gods through him. While lauding and glorifying Agni, the rishis praised him as the possessor of great wealth. The Vedic civilisation believed in performing the 'Yajna' (Fire) ritual twice daily to please the Gods— to get what they wanted in the form of blessings from heaven.

Does Agni give us wealth or knowledge?

Some scholars translate the last word of the above mantra as 'the giver of wealth.' The present-day Vedic scholars do not like this interpretation. Because, after the Vedic period, the ritualistic practices slowly gave way to the

Upanishadic values. The Upanishads started giving the philosophical essence of the Vedas with a mild reprimand for those who overindulge in ceremonial practices. For the salvation of the self, the Upanishads declare that knowledge of ultimate reality or Brahman is essential. The proponents also believed that rituals are only for beginners on the path of realising the ultimate truth. According to them, fire worship alone is insufficient for attaining 'Moksha.'

Rituals Vs Philosophy

During the Vedic period, the clergymen were busy drafting the Brahmanas and the Aranyakas to prescribe the right ways of conducting separate fire worship practices for the commoners and rishis residing in forests. Some must have seen the futility of spending the entire day in fire worship. Therefore, they composed the Upanishads, giving the philosophical essence of the Vedas. It is the uniqueness of the ancient civilisation of the Indian subcontinent—that they accepted new ideas with open minds. Therefore, though the Rigvedic mantras did not change, their meanings changed over the years. Abrahamic faiths never allowed self-correction. The self-correcting characteristic of Indic philosophy is unique in the pantheon of the religious world. That is the secret of sustenance of Vedic Culture in India, which is alive and kicking, even today, despite upheavals in the last four thousand and five hundred years.

Interpretations Suit the Broader Structure

Another unique nature of the Vedic culture was that the rishis did not snub even the Charvakas or the non-believers. On the contrary, Vedanthis engaged with them in philosophical discussions wholeheartedly. Whenever the ritualistic practices were overdone, the wise ones were generally used to intervening and showing the right way. The course correction used to happen very smoothly. Though the Vedas did not change their content, worship methods changed now and then. The interpretations of the Vedas also changed according to the demands of society. Accordingly, the usage and meanings of Vedic Sanskrit words have changed. It helped the evolution of new and contrarian variations. However, the different connotations of the epic fit very well in the structure.

Multiple Sets of Meanings

Modern Vedantic scholars claim that the Rigvedic mantras have multiple meanings, and straightforward definitions are one way to view them. They claim that the mantras' inner explanations and deeper elucidations are possible only to the learned ones.

To understand the different versions of the first mantra, scholars tell us to examine the other meanings of the first two words. "Agnimile Purohitam" may mean "I laud/glorify Agni, the high priest," at first glance. But five different 'Agnis' are burning inside every human being and they control people's lives. And they are named 'Prana,' 'Apana,' 'Vyana,' 'Samana' and 'Udana.'

Likewise, 'Purohitam' combines 'Pura' and 'Hita.' Depending on the context, 'Pura' may refer to 'a town' and 'our body.' The term 'Hita' gives the meaning of 'welfare.' On a cursory look, the verse ends with 'Ratnadatamam,' which offers a sense of "the possessor or giver of great wealth." But the most significant wealth of humanity is 'knowledge' and not any material wealth. Hence, scholars claim that the mantra prays Agni to reveal the ultimate knowledge for the welfare of the people.

The Philosopher's Take on the First Mantra

Therefore, the deeper meaning of the first verse becomes, "I laud the fire Gods, who are active inside me, take care of my body and inner divinity, nourish the world and reveal to us immense knowledge (of ultimate reality)." It makes perfect sense if presented with the word's etymology and phonetics as it is understood in the present day. Vedantic scholars further claim that we must ignore kings and wars in the poems as they do not have significant value. They argue that the battles in the epic only refer to a tussle between good and evil or light and darkness. Max Muller exclaimed, "The Rigveda is the world's first poetry" for its unique ability to throw different meanings according to the readers' taste.

Thus, hymns of all the chapters of the RV generally begin with elaborate praise of the 'Devata' (God or Goddess) of that particular Sukta. In these praises, the author rishi of the particular hymn repeats the mythological stories of that era.

Other Gods in the Rigveda

Vedic scholars have counted thirty-three names of Gods in the text, and a few have a wrong notion that there are thirty-three crore Gods in the Hindu tradition. Out of these thirty-three Devatas, we have seen the importance given to two mighty Gods, namely Indra and Agni. Let us now turn our attention to other Gods occupying the central place in the mantras of the Rigveda.

No other religious text can boast of being as romantic and practical as the Rigvedic chants. The important thing we must bear in mind is that the rishis were keen observers, and they composed mantras about what they had seen. They observed how fire behaved, how the dawn felt, the pleasant sensation that the rising sun gives to the human body, how thunder, lightning, wind and water wreak havoc in people's lives, etc. They have recorded these observations in a poetic format— exaggerating them in a true poet's spirit. The Vedic Gods and Goddesses bear a striking resemblance to these natural forces.

Goddess Ushas

The Goddess of dawn, Ushas, was a beautiful young maiden for the Vedic rishis. They never hesitated to describe her physical attributes. They relate to her beauty and exclaim: "Hey…Look at Ushas, she is like a bathing beauty, now standing up," says one rishi, while the other compares her with a dancer and says, "Usha is like a dancer, and when she peeps out in the horizon she comes dancing around." The latter praise indicates the rishi's observation of the sun's disc early in the morning, which looks like a gyrating or a twirling wheel, fully decked in vibrant colours. Another rishi chants, "She is like a girl, well-groomed by her mother."

A young rishi tells us, "The lovestruck morning sun (Savitr) chases the beautiful maiden (Ushas) relentlessly every day, like a young boy chasing a beautiful girl."

On the contrary, an adult poet praises her, "(Hey…) She is like a mother, who comes out first in the morning and gives birth to the rising sun. Salutations to her," on a sober note. Thus, mantras in the Rigveda are a mixed bag and draw your attention to their various emotions. There are plenty of misconceptions and fears about the text. There is nothing to fear—one must read the text for its poetic grandeur and imagination alone.

At the end of long cold nights, before the first rays of the sun hit the earth, the environment looked beautiful, charged with expectations that energised the people struggling to come out of their slumber. Therefore, they must have started worshipping this magical energy (twilight). They called her Goddess 'Ushas' or 'Usha.' The famous laudatory verse praising 'Savitr' (of the Gayatri mantra) is the worship of the scintillating rising sun. The stress of the Rigveda on Ushas and Savitr made Lokmanya Tilak think that the homeland of the Vedic people was somewhere in the Arctic region.

The Legend of Pusan

Pusan represents the morning sun, which appears on the horizon after the Goddess of dawn, Ushas. In many places in the Rigveda, the morning sun is also called Savitr. Sayana tells us that Pusan is the brother of Ushas. In the Rigveda (RV 1.184.3), the Asvins are none other than Pusan. His primary function is to give protection on the roads. The rishi pleads with Pusan (RV 1.42.1–3) and asks him to chase the lurking wolves and thieves from the paths ahead of them. He is the guardian of every course (RV 6.53.1) and a guide. Pusan has the power to find the lost articles, cattle, etc., and he can trace the hidden goods (6.48.15). He is 'Pasupa' to many as he protects cattle (6.58.2) and goats (Ajasra) pull his chariot (6.55.4).

Varuna, the God of the Heavenly Stream

Varuna's abode is in the sky, as has been reflected in the scripture. He disposes of the heavenly streams and allows them to flow towards the earth. Interestingly, the verses also praise Indra as a rain giver, who controls water flow from above, and he releases water rescued by him from the demons. Therefore, the rishis give equal importance to Indra and Varuna as they generally appear together in many mantras.

"We invoke you, first of all, Oh, Indra and Varuna. Give us blessings and riches," chants the RV 1.17.3.

"Oh, Indra-Varuna, you both are mighty and rich, one of you is called a Monarch and the other an Autocrat," praises RV 7.82.2.

RV 7.82.5 goes one step further by saying, "Oh, Indra and Varuna, you are the creators of the world, and in the time of peace and quiet, Mitra remains with you. The Mighty One goes to battle with the Maruts."

Even Gods fight each other!

The rishi poet, Vamadeva curiously chants about the rivalry between the two powerful Gods of the Rigveda. The Hymn Forty-two of the fourth Mandala brings out the power struggle between Varuna and Indra:

"The kingdom is mine! All the warriors, all immortals are mine. Even the Gods follow Varuna's will. I will rule over the nations with their bodies," declares Varuna and adds, "I hold the highest celestial power." Saying this, he challenges Indra.

Not to be outdone, Indra retorts, "Even Tvaster knows the power of my weapon, Thunder," and reminds Varuna of all his conquests over demons and calls for a showdown.

However, in the concluding parts of the hymn, the rishi soothes the twin power centres and praises both deities eloquently. This hymn is curious because of its undertones. Rishi Vamadeva seems to pacify different poets of the Rigveda to settle their dispute about Indra and Varuna's supremacy.

Varuna also appears in the Rigveda to discipline the rogues in society, and he curses harmful elements with a disease called 'Jalodara.' It may be a waterboarding of the present justice system, and Varuna becomes the deity representing water in the later days.

However, in RV 10.124, the rishi talks bravely about Indra's prominence and Varuna's decline. Even Lord Agni forsakes Varuna for Indra, though reluctantly.

Role of the Asvins

The Asvins were go-to deities for distressed people who later became Gods with wonder drugs to cure ailments. In the Rigveda, the Asvins (the twin Gods) rescued people in anxiety. They saved Bujyu, who was stranded in the middle of the ocean. People who fell into pits were helped by them too. Bhadrimati, a barren woman, gave birth to a child with the blessings of the Asvins. They gave a metal leg to the handicapped Vishpala, a horse so that she could run. A long list of people got help from the Asvins. This pair of Gods were later known as the excellent medical men of their era.

The Group of Adityas and the Visvedevas

The names of the Adityas pop up here and there in the Rigveda (RV). The chief of them is Varuna, and their mother is Aditi. In RV 2.27.1, six of them appear—Mitra, Aryaman, Bhaga, Varuna, Daksa and Amsa, and Surya is the seventh one. Curiously Indra's name does not appear here.

Similarly, the Visvedevas are invoked in many hymns. They are a narrow group associated with Ushas and the Adityas (storm Gods), usually under the leadership of Indra. The mix and match of different sets of Gods and Goddesses throughout the script looks like the preference of individual poets over time.

Goddesses in the RV

The prominent Goddesses that appear in the RV are Ushas and Sarasvati. Apart from them, 'Vac' (goddess of speech—RV 10.71), Prithvi (earth goddess—RV 5.84), Ratri (night goddess—10.127); Aranyani (forest goddess—RV 10.146), Agnayi (Agni's wife); Indrani and Varunani (spouses of Indra and Varuna), make their appearances. However, during the Vedic period, the popular Goddesses of the modern era, Lakshmi and Parvathi, have yet to show up. Goddess Ila and Mahi (Bharathi) were the important family deities of the Puru kings who were the protagonists of the Rigveda.

As Indians had Goddesses in their pantheon of deities during the Rigvedic period, you can call them the world's first women deities.

The Sun God

Apart from different forms of the sun, namely, Ushas, Pusan, Savitr, Aditya, etc., the Sun God also makes an independent appearance in the RV. 'Surya Sukta' praises the Sun God by saying, "Hey, Surya, the moment you appear on the horizon, two things disappear. First and foremost, the stars will disappear, no doubt, and then the thieves, who were active in the night would run away as soon as the first rays hit the earth." These kinds of praises are ubiquitous in the text.

Many believe that the Sun God became Lord Vishnu during the later Vedic period.

What are the main objectives of the verses?

The Rigvedic verses contain many mantras praising the Vedic Gods and Goddesses. The mantras' main deities were Indra, Agni, Varuna, Savitr, Mitra, Adityas, Ushas,

Asvins and Soma. Even today, the regions around the state of Bihar perform the 'Chath Puja,' which worships the Sun God. This ritual comes from the Rigvedic period. Likewise, the mantras from the Vivaha (marriage) Sukta are chanted during marriage ceremonies in modern India. Like any other religious scripture, the verses discuss dos and don'ts for a happy married life.

The rishis firmly believed that the Gods and Goddesses expect sacrificial offerings and Soma oblations with the chant of praises. As a result, they thought that the Gods would bless the people who performed the fire rituals with proper oblations and would give them riches in cattle, grains and good rains. The Vedic people assumed that if they did not undertake this ritual daily, the Gods would get annoyed and curse the populace with ill health and material loss. This belief system existed throughout the known world of the era with tiny variations.

***

3

Tantalising Episodes from the Rigveda

On a cursory glance at the text, we can see that this scripture was a study material in ancient days because it contains mantras to worship various deities and includes moral stories, ethical sermons, puzzles to ponder for young minds, tips on social behaviour and many other social, economic and political issues. The scripture has input on all the relevant matters related to the cradle-to-grave situations of the Vedic era.

We also notice that the Rigveda Samhita's tenth Mandala details many episodes that give a different tone to the collection. While the older Mandalas mainly contained praises of the Vedic deities, the tenth Mandala takes a very candid approach, thus giving us many versions of 'the Creator, the Created and the Creation.' The stories in these verses give us a definite clue about the belief system prevailing during the period.

The Story of Incest (RV 10.10)

In the tenth Hymn of the tenth Mandala of the Rigveda, a disturbing story of Yama and his twin sister, Yami appears. It shocks the ordinary readers but points out what used to happen during the Vedic period. These verses are in the form of a dialogue between a twin brother and a sister.

In this hymn, Yami, overcome by the physical urge after attaining puberty, invites her brother for sex. In reply, Yama tells her, "I know what is happening elsewhere, but I do not like sex between the same bloodline. The Gods see everything."

Not to be outwitted easily, Yami tells her brother, "Look, Prajapathi (Creator) joined us together in the womb. Even the Gods performed sins in the past and nothing is shameful. Do not worry and behave naturally."

She adds, "I am eager to sleep with you and offer my body as the wife would do."

For this atrocious (by present-day moral code) demand made by his twin sister, Yama tells her to find another man and get sexual pleasure from him. What he tells her next is very interesting, "The time has come to prohibit the marriage between a brother and a sister."

This story suggests that the marriages between brothers and sisters happened during the early Vedic period. And perhaps, the rishis wanted to stop this practice with the help of this Hymn.

Conversation between Agastya and Lopamudra (RV 1.179)

The rishis of the Vedic period had wives. They were like commoners—except their primary interest was finding the Ultimate Reality. For the sake of inner awakening, they undertook intense meditation regularly.

Rishi Agastya was an important hermit in the Vedic era. He, too, was eager to gain ultimate knowledge by meditating for long hours. In this quest, he even neglected his newly married wife, Lopamudra. Though initially, Lopamudra took care of her husband, who was busy with his esoteric studies, her patience ran out one day. She decided to raise issues with her husband.

The conversation between the husband and wife appears in the first four verses of hymn one hundred and seventy-nine of the first Mandala. Though this comes as a first chapter of the scripture, the mantras compiled here are clubbed with the tenth chapter as they were composed during the later Vedic period.

Lopamudra: "Do you know how many years have passed since our marriage? I have taken care of you so far, but do you know I have my desires? You have forgotten your wife. You are devoted to your studies! I can wait, but my youthfulness cannot wait! What are your plans? I am just bringing this up to your notice!"

This direct reference must have shocked Agastya beyond imagination. He fumbles in response.

Agastya: "Don't worry. Your efforts are not in vain. You took care of me when I was meditating upon the

Ultimate Reality. The blessings of the Gods are upon both of us. Let's now unite and have the progeny."

Rishi Agastya's student, who overheard the conversation, records this dialogue with his commentary in the last two verses. This hymn indicates women's empowerment in the Vedic period and tells us that husband and wife had an equal say in family matters in the Vedic period. It is strange now. Perhaps, it was natural in those times—that a Peeping Tom's account comes in the scripture as an appropriate reminder to the overzealous rishis.

Gambler's Advice (Aksha Sukta—RV 10.34)

It may sound funny, but it is true. The tenth Mandala contains an entire Sukta (Number thirty-four) dedicated to the professional gambler's advice.

He tells us at the beginning, "The rattling sound of dice excites me like the taste of the Soma drink."

He shamelessly continues, "Though my wife was patient with me, I deserted her for the sake of dice."

"Now, my mother-in-law hates me. My wife shuns me. I am like a beggar and cannot enjoy the game anymore. I feel like a valuable horse grown old."

Perhaps, he realises that it is too late for him. Therefore, he gives his wisdom to others.

"The Gambler's wife becomes the winner's delight. Beware—his father, mother and brothers will say, 'We don't know him. Take him bound anywhere you want.' He continues, 'It's difficult to shrug off the attraction of dice once the greed of the game pins you down.'"

The Dice Game in Progress

"The Sun God told me a secret—to shun the game and engage in agriculture. Pay serious attention to my advice. Do not gamble. Instead, pursue agriculture which will give you cattle, wife and other riches."

The last (fourteenth mantra) verse is a prayer to the dice— "Be a friend to us. Bring happiness and don't show your wrath on us. Let your anger fall on our enemies and let them plunge under the bondage of brown dice."

Its composer has beautifully and meaningfully crafted this hymn. The hymn contains a complete lesson to the gambler about what will happen if he continues with his vice. This Vedic advice holds good even for the modern gambler. The hymn reflects societal ills, such as gambling and drinking in the ancient era, which most rishis tried to end. Interestingly, the dice game brings a never-ending stream of miseries to the Pandavas in the Mahabharata story. Strangely, Yudishtira, the eldest brother of Pandavas, knew all the Vedas well but failed to adhere to the advice. Unfortunately, the saga continues to date without any sign of cessation. The basic instinct of human beings to get rich quickly is on the rise rather than diminishing.

The most exciting thing is that Kavasha Ailusha, the author of Aksha Sukta, is described as the son of an enslaved woman. He was a professional gambler before composing the hymn. Yet, he was one of the rishis of the Rigveda because of this Sukta. Ancient rishis never bothered about the social status of the people who composed the verses before incorporating mantras into the text. The editor, Shakala, accepted the poems—

irrespective of who composed them—if the content suited the reader.

Jnana Sukta (RV 10.71)

This hymn tells us about the rishis assembled to discuss how to name things and objects. They use the simile of separating the flour and chaff using the sieve. The mantra explains that the rishis discussed thoroughly, removing the trash from the flour using their heart and mind as excellent filters to get the right way to name physical objects. This episode explains how words and language were created and understood in Vedic times. This Sukta also tells you that "The knowledge is walking towards you (continuously). Some do not see it, and some—though they see and hear it, do not understand it. However, for some, the speech or Vak (also refers to knowledge) reveals her lovely form like a finely-robed wife revealing herself to her loving husband."

Vedic rishis gave a lot of importance to 'Vak Shuddhi.' Therefore, they discuss the importance of purity (Shuddhi) of Vak or speech. Goddess Sarasvati becomes Vagdevi (Vak+devi) in later years.

Did sages fight amongst them?

The rivalry between Vishwamithra and Vasista comes out ferociously in the third and seventh Mandalas. The RV records the verbal missiles fired against each other. Vishwamithra openly challenges Vasista by saying, "Do you know what? This Vashista won the war (Dasharajnya war) by using black magic."

Vasista retorts, "If at all I used black magic, let the Gods curse me with immediate death."

There are Puranic stories about the infamous enmity between otherwise sober rishis. The fight continues even in the present-day situation, where a Vasista Gotra boy cannot marry a girl from the Vishwamithra Gotra and vice versa.

Manyu Sukta (RV 10.83 and 10.84)

Unlike modern philosophers, the Vedic rishis believed that anger is the essential prerequisite for human survival. They prayed and invited 'Manyu' (temper, anger or passion) to station permanently on their right arm so that the worshippers could conquer wealth and treasure by slaying the enemies. Fourteen verses of the above Suktas praise the virtues of 'Anger.' In his chant, the rishi equates anger to Indra, Varuna and all other virtuous Gods and pleads with them to give strength and vigour to the weak man. Why not? In those days of turmoil and violence, the will to kill the enemy was necessary. Only such people emerged victorious in battles.

Varuna Sukta (RV 7.86)

Vasista excels in his poetry in the seventh Mandala. Sanskrit scholar, Dr. Sucheta Paranjape describes him as the greatest poet of the Rigveda. Vasista had written this Sukta specifically to please Varuna (water God), who was angry at him. Vasista, when told by some rishis that Varuna (Vasista claims that Varuna is his father) is mad at him, realises that he has stopped talking to him. Then the rishi approaches Varuna and implores him by saying, "Hey, Varuna, what happened to the bond between us, which was so vibrant? I remember you took me once to your palatial house with a thousand doors which were so huge. I also recall a boat ride you took me in and I felt as if I was in a swing."

He does not stop there and continues, "I know you are angry with me." The gem of a mantra comes here, where he says, "If you are angry because of what I said, I would like to clarify," and gives four reasons why such a thing must have happened like any other kid talking to his parent.

"If at all I said something wrong about you, it should have happened under the influence of 'Sura' (liquor) or when I was mad at something or when I was playing dice or when I was out of my mind."

He lists four reasons for blurting out something irritating, which holds good even in the current situation. Look at the boldness of the rishi in conceding his habits rather than hiding them. Not only that, these mantras also suggest that these vices were not frowned upon during the Vedic era. Such episodes make the characters appearing in the RV very humane. This Sukta was chanted to atone for one's sins in the Vedic age.

Manduka Sukta (RV 7.103)

In this Sukta, Vasista ridicules those who chant the Vedas blindly by following a lead priest. It is a supreme parody where he exclaims, "A manduka (frog) sleeps like a leather bag for a year, gets up once the rain starts and croaks in tune with the lead frog. Some chant the Vedas like a black frog, white frog or grey frog—in copying the leader. Similarly, some recite the Vedas blindly, following the main priest. What is the use of such chants?"

Look at the authority and courage that Vasista had to construct a mantra like this, which criticises his creed by ridiculing them, stating that they are like frogs if they chant the Vedas without understanding it. Rishi Shakala, the chief editor, dared to include this Sukta in his Samhita. The simile used here is amazingly stunning and beautiful at the same time.

Cart Race in the Rigveda (RV 10.102)

It is worth understanding what Vedic people aspired for, apart from a long and healthy life. A Sukta in the tenth Mandala of the Rigveda tells us a story of an aged rishi and his young wife. Mudgala, the rishi, wanted to compete in a cart race and win a handsome prize announced by the sponsors. He went to Indra and requested that he modify his old cart into a lighter, more modern chariot. Indra obliged, pleased by Mudgala's praises and offerings.

But Mudgala was too old to drive the modified coach himself. No problem—his young wife, Mudgalani, readily drove the chariot with aplomb and won the race. The prize was one thousand heads of cattle. The herds of cattle were considered the most significant wealth in those days, along with granaries full of grains. The gold plates covering the horns of the cattle, which were won in the race came as a bonus. King Janaka of Videha announced a similar prize to the wisest man in his court, as detailed in the Brihadaranyaka Upanishad's story.

However, some argue that this hymn was chanted at the time of 'Niyoga.' A substitute for an impotent or dead husband was appointed in the Niyoga ritual. Here, they claim the actual race is for virility and fertility. The prize is an offspring. The cart driven by a bull wins the race in the story, and the deity invoked is Indra. Mudgalani is the young wife of old Rishi Mudgala. To top it all, the rishi of the hymn is none other than Mudgala. This episode is quite a mind-blowing one which innocently comes into the script. We all know that the Niyoga practice comes extensively in the Mahabharata epic.

Soma Mandala (RV 9)

The ninth book, or Mandala (114 hymns), is devoted to chanting the Vedic elixir, Soma's praises. The very first mantra clarifies that the drink is for Indra.

> "Purify yourself across the filter at speed Soma, when we press thee for Indra to drink"

> "The daughter of the Sun purifies circling Soma with the woollen filter in unfailing measure."

> "Indra, the champion, keeps smashing all obstacles and bestows bounties in the explosion of just this (Soma). "

Thus, in the first hymn, the rishi tells us that the Soma is crushed along with cow's milk and passed through the woollen filters to prepare it for Indra to drink. After drinking this sacred potion, Indra explodes with energy, smashes all the enemies and distributes wealth.

"Purify yourself across the filter at speed, Soma-pursuing the Gods,

As a bull, enter Indra, oh, drop."

The second hymn begins with the urging of Soma to speed up through the filters and enter Indra to make him a bull. It indirectly refers to Indra's battlefield aggression and sexual prowess.

"Oh, drop, you are cow-winning, man-winning, horse-winning and prize-winning. You are the ancient embodiment of the sacrifice."

The last mantra praises Soma for all the battles won and informs us that Soma is very potent.

"Bring us glittering wealth in horses. Oh, drop, through our whole lifetime. Then make us better off."

Thus, the ninth Mandala continuously chants the mantras to praise Soma until the end.

But, shockingly, we are yet to learn what this Soma is. Is it a plant? Is it a root? Is it a shrub? Is it a flower? Or is it a bud? It is a mystery that Indians never wanted to unravel more after its usage declined in performing the rituals.

Nevertheless, we find the mention of this drink in all the Mandalas without exception, apart from the 'Soma Mandala.' It has an overpowering presence in the text.

Maybe Soma's strong presence in the RV attracted the attention of the Westerners if not Indians. Many tried to identify this plant with the help of markers left behind by the rishis describing its attributes in the hymns.

Is It Ephedra?

S. Mahdihassan has made serious attempts to prove that the Chinese plant, Ephedra's juice is Soma. He informs us that the drink is good for longevity, and a drop used to be given to the newborn—a Vedic custom which was copied by the Romans. The Rigveda called Soma 'golden yellow.' The Ephedra plant has yellow stalks. He further claims that the equivalent word for Soma in Chinese means 'Fire-yellow fibres of hemp.' In the illustration of the plant that he gives with its stalks, which are straight and rod-like, it looks like an arrow—as has been described in the RV.

Or Fly-Agaric?

But, the most exciting article I found on the subject is by Gorden Wassen, which was presented at the Congress of Orientalists, Canberra, Australia in 1971. He has studied the Mandala in detail and culled out the descriptions of the Soma which have been given in the verses. He provides the details of these mantras with their translations by the scholars to conclusively prove that it is 'a mushroom jetting out of the earth.' He informs us that the mushroom's name is Fly-Agaric (Toadstool), and the Shamanic tribes of Siberia used them until recently for their religious purposes.

Although he also experimented with the Ephedra plant, he claims that it was introduced later in the ceremonies.

Why did he feel so? He quotes many verses from the ninth Mandala— "He (Soma) has clothed himself with fire-bursts of the sun—(9.71.9)." "He has been cleansed by the sun's rays, (9.76.4)." "He has the single eye (glittering Redcap) (9.97.46). " "Thine, oh, Pavamana, are the lights, the sun—(9.86.29)." It was referred to as the 'Sun Plant' or the 'Fire Plant.' Its stalk looks like a 'pillar of the sky.' The rishis chant that the steeds of the sun, 'Etasa' are a flaming red-yellow, and Soma juice is of the same dazzling colour.

"The hide is of a bull, the dress is of sheep (9.70.7)." Here, the red skin of the Soma plant shows through the woolly tufts remaining on the top of the woollen sieve which is spread across the vessel to collect the juice. It is hiding through the 'dress of sheep' (woollen filter). He describes the compelling metaphor for Soma—'the single eye' of the sacred plant refers to the head or cap of the mushroom (Umbrella-shaped) with dazzling red colour and white dots on it.

When Gorden presents the photographs of the mushrooms with white stalks and a sun-red cap with white dots, it matches the descriptions. You may agree or disagree with him, but the amount of research he has undertaken is enormous.

Preparation of Soma

The Second Filter

The rishis discuss the second filter, that purifies the Soma liquid (9.86.40; 9.66.5; 9.67.22–25). They praise Soma as Agni. The miraculous plant shares the attributes of Lord Agni—flame-coloured, and it purifies by itself like fire does with its flames. Or are they talking about the burning sensation one experiences while drinking Soma? Who can tell us?

The Third Filter

This claim by Gordon is obnoxious. Therefore, he gives a caveat, "We are treading on the holiest ground in the Vedic religion. In every genuine faith, there are acts, objects and words that evoke awe in the believer and elicit a tug at the sinews of his heart. The faithful are then in the presence of a holy mystery. There is a kind of an overwhelming sense of this tremendous reverence, even though we are far removed in time and place."

He quotes Dr. O'Flaherty for giving this rendering—"The swollen men urinate the on-flowing Soma,"—the 'men' being the priests presiding over the Soma sacrifice. The men are swollen, in the opinion of Geldner and Renou, because their bladders are full. So, he concludes that the 'third filter' is the human organism, which converts Soma into potent urine.

The holy man of the Shaman tribe used the Fly-Agaric juice in the neighbouring area of Siberia for drinking before ritual practices and saved his urine. Why? Because this potent hallucinogenic mushroom retains its potency even after passing through the human kidneys. Others drink this urine with an identical inebriating effect. Another reason for this practice is that certain nauseating ingredients in the original mushroom are filtered out through the human. Only people with a robust internal filtering process could bear this juice. The consumption was repeated until it passed through five people. Of course, there is no evidence for this in the text.

However, in the Avesta (Yasna 48.10), Zarathustra angrily denounces those who use inebriating urine in the sacrifice. He angrily shouts, "When wilt thou do away with the urine of drunkenness with which the priests evilly delude the people?"

We cannot forget that the priests from the Anu tribe brought Lord Agni and Soma for fire rituals in the beginning. The Parsis, the descendants of the Zoroastrians, drink a bull's urine in their religious practices in a symbolic way, even today. Hindus consume 'Gomuthra' (cow's urine) on some auspicious days for purification.

In the ancient Vedic times, the life expectancy rate of the people must have been less than forty years, with many uncertainties in day-to-day life. They needed a lot of energy and enthusiasm to lead a normal life. No wonder Soma threw open the portals of ecstasy for them. Whether it is Ephedra or Fly Agaric—that does not matter. But yes, we need to do a lot to discover the mystery of this sacred potion.

Pavamana of the 'Pouranic' Times

When the rituals related to the Soma sacrifice came down slowly after the Vedic era, the ninth Mandala shone in its new avatar. Ignoring the Soma aspects of the sacrifice, the priests started focussing on the purifying attributes of the sacred potion. The Rigvedic poets always used multiple names to address the deities. For the Soma, they substituted 'Pavamana' many times in the verses for that shining yellow liquid that appeared. They chanted very fervently that:

> "Here he is, racing with the sun, Pavamana in the sky." (9.27.5)

> "Pavamana has hitched Etasa (the sun's steed) to the sun." (9.63.8)

> "Flow for our immunity from defeat and slaughter. Flow for our welfare, for the great sacrifice, for all the Gods. All these, my friends, desire this. This I desire. Oh, Soma Pavamana." (9.96.4)

> "You, Soma, are everywhere—the contemplator of men. You, Pavamana, the showerer, hasten to these (waters). Do you pour forth upon us (wealth), comprising various treasures and gold? May we be (able) to live in the worlds." (9.86.38)

Many such praises keep coming in the various Suktas, thus attributing all the traits of the Soma, like dazzling red, all purifying, ability to reach the sun to Pavamana. Slowly, a new meaning to the word emerged. Pavamana appears before us as the Storm God (Maruts), a cleanser of all sins and capable of showering good fortune on the worshippers. Eventually, he becomes the Great Hanuman or Maruthi (son of Maruts). Indians have forgotten the Soma sacrifice. The mantras from the ninth Mandala are now chanted to cleanse the sins or to invoke blessings from Lord Hanuman for better prospects. Does it fit into the structure of the verses eulogising the Pavamana? Yes, it does. Because the mythological God, Hanuman has all those attributes according to the stories.

These evolutions over time intrigue the Westerners to no end, but for the Indian pious population, it is a regular and welcome change—strengthening their beliefs. These subtle changes made the Indian culture more resilient and sustainable for over four thousand years.

The Stone Pressers (RV 7.33)

Significantly, hymn number thirty-three of Mandala Seven is full of self-boasting by the Vasistas. They claim that they are the only ones with hair knots worn on the right side of the head. They talk about the white robes, their unique clothes as Yama spins them, their heavenly birth, etc. Interestingly, they even inform us of the Soma pressers in one of the verses, naming them as the sons of Yayata and Pashadyumna. This verse hints at the importance of the Soma pressers in Vedic society.

Wedding Hymns

The selected verses from the RV 10.85 are invoked even during modern Hindu weddings to bless the couple.

Go to [your new] home, and you are the lady of the house;

Speak out with authority;

Prosper here, loved [and] with children;

In your home, watch over the household;

Join yourself with this husband;

You will address people even when you are old.

It adds, "May you have ten sons and let the eleventh be your husband (in his old age)." "Don't be harsh with your husband. Be kind to all quadrupeds and bipeds of the household. Raise many heroes lovingly. Be fearful of the Gods and bring prosperity and good fortune to your new abode."

These blessings were showered upon all new brides who entered their husbands' houses.

This hymn also tells the story of the new bride (Sun God's daughter) riding into her husband's house (the Moon God is her husband) in a grandly-decked chariot driven by the Asvins and guided by the Adityas.

During the Vedic period, the girls' parents arranged a 'Swayamvara' to facilitate their daughters in selecting a suitable bridegroom for themselves. Women could have remarried if their husbands died or disappeared. A young rishi named Gosha tells us an episode of an elopement (RV 7.55.5–8): "Let my beloved's entire household, including her brothers and other relatives, as well as the dogs, be lulled into a deep sleep so that the lovers (we) could creep out stealthily." The innocent beauty of this epic lies in these tiny little details.

The Vrishakapi Hymn (RV 10.86)

After the wedding hymn, there comes the sexually explicit Vrishakapi hymn. It is appropriate and natural for this Sukta to appear after the wedding hymn. The ancient rishis were candid, practical and celebrated life in its true spirit. The Vedantic scholars influenced by present-day moral codes are greatly embarrassed by the verses of this hymn. Even the European translators of the RV shied away from translating mantras numbering sixteen and seventeen from this hymn. Ralph Griffith did not translate these verses. Another English scholar, H. H. Wilson, circumspected them by vague mentions.

The Rigveda calls the Vrishakapi a companion/son of Indra. What is Vrishakapi? Wilson translates it as a 'great ape.' Shankaracharya defines it as 'one who showers all aspects of desire.' Indra declares that without this ape, he cannot enjoy life. Indrani (Indra's wife) praises Vrishakapi for its prowess and, in the same breath, admonishes it for the pain sustained. Let us look at verse number seven of the hymn:

"Mother, whose love is quickly won, I say what verily will be.
My breast, oh, Mother, and my head and hips seem quivering.
Supreme is Indra overall."

Yes, indeed! You guessed it right. The poem is about the importance of the sexual act and the penetration required for begetting the progeny (Mantra numbering Sixteen and Seventeen). Interestingly, the editor credits Indrani, Indra and Vrishakapi for this Sukta. And no rishi claims credit for the piece. The last verse of the hymn (Number Twenty-three) declares the intentions behind all the mantras— "Manu's daughter, Parshu gave birth to twenty children at once…let all prolific bellies be like that with the blessings of all-mighty Indra." We cannot sit on a judgement about the social ethics and compulsions of Vedic people in the modern era.

Funeral Hymns (RV 10.14–18)

Even death becomes very colourful in these four hymns. One feels safe and protected even after death if one hears these Suktas. The chants invite Yama and his father, Vivaswan, along with deified rishis, such as the Angirasas, the Navagvas, the Atharvanas and the Bhrigus, thus offering them appropriate oblations. In their gracious presence, the body, duly cleansed using the all-purifying waters of river Sarasvati, was offered to Agni for transporting the dead to the destination they deserved. The verses declare that the body consigned to flames need not be buried.

What happens to the buried souls? They had a different set of mantras for them. The RV 10.18.11 goes thus: "Heave thyself earth, nor press thee heavily downward, afford him easy access, gently tending him. Cover him as a mother wraps her sari around her child.

Oh, Earth." (Ralph Griffith). The sensitivity and loving care towards the dead in these verses are adorable.

Like all other ancient people, death was nothing to be scared of but looked upon as a passage to a higher or brighter world.

Metres in the Rigveda and Mysticism

Another aspect that bewilders Western scholars is the metres used in the text. There is no doubt about the antiquity of the RV in their minds. However, it is difficult for them to accept that the Vedic people could set the verses or mantras in a precise order of syllables. Perhaps the question that always lingers in their mind is, "How on earth were the rishis even thinking of using structured syllables in their poems when the whole known world used to struggle with forming proper sentences?" This aspect is another reason why they tend to advance the creation of the 'Vedas' to recent times.

The RV was composed in various Vedic metres. There are mainly seven important metres used in the RV, apart from many others. They are Gayathri, Anustubh, Tristubh, Jagathi, Pankthi, Usnih and Brahathi. Let us avoid getting into the technical details of each of them. Gayathri was the primarily used metre in old Mandalas out of these seven. The famous 'Gayatri mantra' (RV 3.62.10) of Hindu ritualistic tradition is a shining example of the Rigvedic practice—alive and kicking in modern India.

Here, the mysticism of numbers comes into play. For instance, there is an esoteric logic followed when it is argued that the words Bhumi (earth), Antariksa (atmosphere) and Vyoma (sky) are formed in eight syllables. A Gayatri 'pada' (line) consists of eight syllables. Therefore he who knows the Gayatri metre gains the three worlds. The metres are vital in ritual mysticism and are considered divine beings. Even oblations were offered to metres in mythological stories. It is a perfect example of the creative mindset of the epoch.

4

Creation Stories in the Rigveda

The stories of the Creation, Creator and Created play a vital role in religions worldwide. The Bible tells us, "In the beginning, God created the Heaven and the Earth," and that God created the world in six days. Similarly, the Quran states that "Allah created the heavens and the earth and all that is between them in six days." Of course, there are subtle differences between the two stories. However, what is common is that no doubts can be raised in the creation stories mentioned in those scriptures, and the faithful are not to question or alter them.

However, the Rigveda's take on creation is different. Despite what Vedantic scholars claim, the epic of the Rigveda becomes very candid and upright in admitting 'we do not know,' which no other scripture dares to concede.

Such admission comes in hymn number one hundred and twenty-nine of the Tenth Mandala, popularly known as Nasadiya Sukta or the 'Hymn of Creation.' Look at what the sixth verse of this hymn declares:

After all, who knows? Who can say,

From where it all came, and how creation happened?

The Gods themselves are later than creation,

So who knows genuinely from where it has risen?

It does not stop there in its scepticism and goes on and declares:

Where does all creation have its origin?

Whether the Creator made it or whether he did not?

The Creator who surveys from the highest heaven

Does he know—or maybe even he does not know? (RV 10.129.7)

The State of the Universe Before the Creation

All seven verses of the Nasadiya Sukta (RV 10.129) have a contemplative tone, beginning with a statement that "Then there was neither existence nor non-existence" to describe the state of the Universe before Its creation. After that, the hymn raises questions about the creation with humility and an inquiring mind. The tenth Mandala of the Rigveda comes at the end of the epic. Doubts raised here signal the beginning of Vedantic philosophy in the subcontinent.

The ancient rishis claimed that the Vedas were not their creation but were born out of nowhere due to intuitional flash. There is no doubt about the focussed reflective thinking that has gone into composing the verses. Therefore, as claimed by the rishis, it may be apt to term the epic as a creation due to the inspirational thought process by the grace of Gods. All religious scriptures of this world claim that to be so. Even great poets attribute their creations to some unforeseen power.

These kinds of chants are a testimony to the fact that ancient India's wise people, or rishis were very candid. They did not mind saying what they wanted in plain language. Old Rigvedic Mandala chants denote that the rishis knew all about the Gods and Goddesses in heaven. But the later rishis dared to admit that they did not know much about the Creation and the Creator. These chants depict the natural wisdom of rishis with enquiring minds and scientific temperament, which impresses many from the modern era.

The Purusha Sukta (The Rigveda 10.90)

This Sukta grandly announces the Rigvedic concept of 'Universal Consciousness' and the interconnectedness of the Universe. All the world religions have given their version of how the Universe is created and maintained. But, the Rigveda gives multiple views on this controversial issue of creation.

The 'Purusha' mentioned in this Sukta is gender-neutral and has a thousand heads, eyes and feet. "It permeates the Universe on all sides and extends beyond it by ten fingers (figuratively). It is whatever has been and whatever is to be. It is the ruler of immortality when it grows beyond everything through food. All creatures are a quarter of him. Three-quarters are immortals in heaven."

"From it, Viraj (the female creative principle) was born. The verses and the chants were born. The metres were born from it. Horses, cows, goats, sheep and other animals were born. The Brahmanas came from its mouth, the Kshatriyas from its arm, the Vaishyas from its thighs and the Shudras from its feet.

The moon was born from its mind and the sun from its eyes. Indra and Agni came from his mouth. From its vital breath, the wind was born. From its navel, the middle realm of space arose. From its head, heaven evolved. The sky appeared from its ear, and thus, they set the worlds in order."

Thus, the 'Universal Consciousness' descriptions come out brilliantly in the Rigveda.

More on Creation

In the Hiranyagarbha Sukta (The Rigveda 10.121), the Universe emerges from the golden embryo. (The sun?) "In the beginning arose Hiranyagarbha (the golden egg), the Lord of all created beings. He established the earth and heaven and supports them," claims the first mantra. But the mantra does not abandon its candid repartee and ends with, "What God shall we adore with oblation?" (kasmaï devāyả haviṣā ̎ vidhema).

Similarly, though the first nine mantras praise the Creator in many words, funnily, the ending is with the same question, "What God shall we adore with oblation?"

In the last mantra, the rishi addresses the Creator as 'Prajapati' and chants, "You alone comprehend all these created things and none besides you. When we invoke you, grant us our hearts' desire. May we have rich stores of provisions."

The composer of Sukta number 10.72 of the RV was the son of Brahaspati, who praised his father for blowing breath into non-existence to form existence in the early ages of Gods.

Similarly, the deity of Sukta numbered 10.125 of the RV is Vak (Speech) and this hymn is also referred to as Devi Sukta by many. In these verses, Vagdevi (Goddess) proclaims to be the originator of all the Gods and claims that all the existence is living on the earth because of Her billowing breath.

Vishwakarma Sukta

Vishwakarma Sukta (10.81) imagines the creator as an artisan (sculptor, smith, woodcutter or carpenter).

Gayathri Mantra

"We meditate on the adorable glory of the radiant sun; May He inspire our intelligence." (RV 3.62.10)

The above is the most straightforward translation of the famous Gayatri Mantra by equally famous philosopher, S. Radhakrishnan.

The believers chant this verse daily in their ritualistic prayers to God. The Vishwamitras chanted this verse, thus calling upon the disciples to meditate upon the radiant sun as He inspires and guides us in the right direction without glorifying any of the Gods or Goddesses. Mandala Three is one of the oldest chapters of the text. In this Mandala, the significant verses are in Gayathri meter, including the pristine Gayathri mantra.

Despite multiple creation stories propounded by the text, there is a caveat in the Rigveda (1.164), which points out that there is 'only one reality' (or 'one truth' or 'one being') which rishis praise as many ('Ekam Sat Vipra Bahudha Vadanti'). That is the strength of the text and not a weakness because it is always open for the ultimate truth to emerge from the various debates and discussions.

It is fascinating to note how these ideas about the Creation and the Creator developed further in the Upanishadic era. The following four sayings quote the Rigveda as resource material.

'Pragyanam Brahman,' or 'Consciousness (the Real knowledge) is the Ultimate Truth,' proclaims Aitareys Upanishad, a part of the Rigveda. Brihadaranyaka Upanishad (part of Yajurveda) takes it to a different level when it grandly states, 'Aham Brahmasmi' or 'I am Brahman.' Chandogya Upanishad (part of Sama Veda) supports this and thunders 'Tatvam Asi' or 'You are That (the Ultimate Truth).' Manduka Upanishad (part of the Atharva Veda) says the same thing differently— 'Ayamatma Brahma' or 'This Soul is Brahman.'

Charvaka Darshana

Remarkably, wise people from the Vedic era gave equal honours to the Charvakas, the class atheists. Though they did not accept the sayings in the Vedas, they studied them well before rejecting them. The Nasadiya Sukta must have inspired them. They refused to believe anything which could not be verified here and now. They questioned, "If we can satiate the Gods in heaven by oblations, why can't we serve food to the people sitting on the first floor from the ground floor without going up?"

With their sharp wit, they asked ritualists, "If the animal sacrificed in the Yajna ritual goes to heaven, why can't the doer offer his father in place of the animal?" Their advice to the people was, "You are born to enjoy life, and there is nothing left after death. How can the burnt body return to life?" They outrightly rejected the existence of a soul other than the body. But, their goal was to find the Ultimate Truth like any of the other rishis.

✳✳✳

5

River Sarasvati and the Rigveda

Sarasvati is a Goddess and the most revered river in the Rigveda. It is a belief that the Rigvedic Mandalas were composed on the banks of this sacred river. Perhaps that is why Sarasvati is invoked seventy-five times in the Rigveda Samhita. She was a river and a Goddess. In later years, she finally turns into a Goddess of education and wisdom when the river loses its importance as a mighty river. Rishi Gṛtsamada says in the RV 2.41.16:

> "Oh, best of mothers! Oh, best of rivers! Oh, best of Goddesses! Sarasvati! We are without any accomplishments or knowledge. Please, Mother, make us accomplished and wise!"

So, one can see Goddess Sarasvati has been prayed to for knowledge and wisdom since the Vedic times. The above mantra is fully equivalent to the classical prayers that are popular today, such as:

"सरस्वति नमस्तुभ्यं वरदे कामरूपिणि । विद्यारम्भं करिष्यामि सिद्धिर्भवतु मे सदा ॥"

"(Oh, Sarasvati, giver of boons and who is multifaceted, we salute you. (My child is) commencing education. Make it fruitful always."

Several mantras express this fervent prayer to Sarasvatī for wisdom and knowledge at the beginning of a child's education. The Rigvedic poets also attributed many other tributes to her in their chants:

RV 1.3.10:

"Sarasvati, the great purifier, full of energy and riches, the source and giver of our riches, may she conduct our yajna with richness."

RV 1.3.11:

"The inspirer of deep spiritual truths, and the impeller of wise minds, Sarasvati has carried the yajna."

RV 1.3.12:

"The great ocean (mass of water), Sarasvati, inspired by her brilliance. She illuminates all minds."

RV 1.13.9:

"Iḷa, Sarasvati and Mahi, the three Goddesses who bring welfare and prosperity—may the immortal ones take their seat on the sacred grass."

RV 1.188.8:

"Oh, Bharati, Iḷa and Sarasvati, as I am fervently praying to you, please let us be inspired into the prosperity of all kinds."

RV 6.61.4:

"Goddess Sarasvati, full of energy and riches, the protector of intellects, may She safe guard us."

Goddess Ila and Mahi were the important family deities of Puru kings who were the protagonists of the Rigveda. Goddess Sarasvati commanded equal status which was at par with the family deities. This indicates the river's importance during the Vedic times.

Sarasvati, the Mighty River:

"She breaks up the rocks on her banks with her mighty waves, digging up the mud for lotus roots. She quickly destroys things from a great distance (with her powerful and voluminous flow). To that Sarasvatī, we offer our prayers and beautiful words for protection and prosperity." (RV 6.61.2)

Sarasvati was the early Vedic people's biggest and most significant river, as represented in the Rigveda Samhita. The sixth Maṇḍala invokes only Sarasvati and none of the rivers to its west. The sixth Maṇḍala has been universally acknowledged as the oldest part of the extant Rigveda Samhita by even Western Indologists, such as Oldenberg. This fact has been brilliantly incorporated by Shrikant Talageri to indisputably demonstrate that the native place of the Vedic people was on the banks of river Sarasvati and that there are no memories left behind in the text about the western rivers. The river, Ganga is mentioned four times in the entire Ṛigveda Samhita—once in the Nadisukta (10.75) and once as a derivative (gangeyah) in the RV 6.45.31, and twice as Jahnavi (3.58.6, 1.116.19).

So we can see that the sixth Maṇḍala, the oldest part of the Ṛigveda Samhita, knows Ganga as well as Sarasvati, but none of the rivers further west, such as Sutudri, Vipaṭ, Asikni, Sindhu, etc. If the Aryan invasion/migration occurred, they would have had to cross all those rivers before encountering Sarasvati or Ganga, and one of those rivers would have been sacred due to more familiarity. Since the oldest part of the Ṛigveda Samhita only knows these two rivers, it is clear that the earliest native place of the Vedic people centres on the banks of Sarasvati around Kurukshetra and its downstream areas.

The above discussions indirectly prove that the Vedic people settled on the banks of the river Sarasvati and sang these chants which have been incorporated in the Rigvedic text. But we cannot rule out that they have crossed all the western rivers before entering and settling down in the Sarasvati valley, as the scientists claim that we all have migrated from Africa to various places. It is only to suggest that the Vedic people completely forgot the other rivers because they settled in the river belt for hundreds of years, if not thousands of years, by the time of composing chants of praises.

Nadi Suktas (RV 3.33 and RV 10.75)

There are plenty of Akhyana Suktas or Samvada Suktas (twenty-one stories appear in a dialogue format) in the RV- the story of Pururavas and Urvashi, the Sarama episode, etc. Nadi Suktas belong to this category.

Like all other hymns, the thirty-third Sukta of Mandala Three is crisp and gives us the bare minimum information about an episode. These mantras were composed by the Vishwamitras. Rishi Vishwamitra arrives with the victorious king, Bharatha (it does not give us any details of the victory) on the banks of two rivers, Vipas and Satudri (present-day Beas and Sutlej) and starts praising these rivers.

"Hey, beautiful rivers. You are like two horses running together. You are like a cattle and her calf…"

He praises the rivers because he intends to cross them with the king and his army. The rivers retort, "Hey, Brahmin, why do you praise us so much? What do you want? Make it clear to us—don't beat around the bush."

Then, Rishi Vishwamithra humbly submits to the rivers and says, "I salute you great rivers. My people are tired, and we want to cross the rivers. Would you please lower the water for us to cross over?"

"Okay. But then, what would you give us in return? Why should we do that for you?"

"Tell me, what can I do for you?"

"You claim to be a great poet! Why don't you write some Suktas and include our name in those poems so that we can become immortal."

Vishwamithra agrees, but rivers are no easy pushovers. "You know what, Indra's command binds us. He ordered us to flow continuously. We can't oblige you."

Vishwamitra does not give up so easily. He persists by saying, "I will write two more Suktas for you—praising your greatness. Please allow us a safe passage," and the haggling continues. In the end, the rivers relent. The above translations are loosely done, catching the spirit of the conversations between the rishi and the rivers. But verses number Five and Six have something special to tell us.

In verse number Five, Vishwamithra tells the rivers, "Hey, rivers charged with waters, rest for a moment from your course at my request—who is going to gather Soma (plant)? I, the son of Kushika desirous of protection, address you with earnest prayers—especially to the rivers before me."

Watch out for what rivers tell him in reply— "Indra, the wielder of the thunderbolt, dug our channels when he slew Ahi (Vritra), the blocker-up of waterways. The divine and well-handed Savitr (morning sun) has had us (on our path), and obedient to his command, we flow as ample (stream)." (Translations by Horace Wilson).

Vishwamithra Praising Rivers

When we read the above verses closely, we get two important indicators. Vishwamithra tells the rivers that his party is proceeding in search of the sacred Soma plants. They travel from the banks of Sarasvati, taking a northwestern route to secure the plant, and rivers do not get offended by their plans. This passage shows the importance of the Soma extracts in the Vedic period.

Secondly, and most importantly, the remark of the rivers that Indra's thunderbolt dug their channels and the reference to the slaying of the demon, Vritra, perhaps point to the changing of the courses of the rivers in those days. Rishis knew that these rivers from the mountains altered their courses frequently due to the vagaries of environmental changes and the tremors felt in the region.

Historians claim that the devastating famine on one side and the invaders on the other destroyed once-great Sumerian cities, such as Ur and Uruk. The people were forced to flee to the northern Akkadian region, leaving behind their southern homeland in the fertile crescent.

The seashore retreated from the city of Ur, and so did the Euphrates by changing its course, thus slowly and steadily ebbing life from a once glorious land. Scholars claim that the Sumerian civilisation vanished from the face of the earth by 1700 BCE. Unfortunately, though they invented writing on clay tablets in human history, we do not have their versions for all the evil things that happened to their cities. However, a couple of tablets with stories of the devastation of the cities survived.

But for the Vedic people, the changes are due to divine interventions. Their reasoning for all the upheaval was Indra's slaying of Vritra. In those days, it was the duty of the rishis to interpret the visible happenings. The mythical stories were the best tools for the priestly class in that era worldwide. We are open to spinning stories of these kinds, even in the modern age. The earthquakes in river basin areas changing many river beds (as proposed by the archaeologists) of northern India were spun into impressive heavenly stories by the rishis.

Nadi Sukta (RV 10.75)

The scripture's tenth Mandala is the last to be composed in the series. Yet another Nadi Sukta appears here, and the rivers are the deities of the Sukta. Coincidently, the composer's name of this hymn is Sindukshit. Why do I say this? Because by this time of the mature period of Vedic culture, the rishis were aware of the complete geography of the Indo-Sarasvati civilisation area. They came to know that the river Sindhu was mightier than the river Sarasvati. They started naming the rishis by the name 'Sindhu'—like the poet of this hymn.

In this hymn, the rivers were named from east to west in perfect order. Mantra number Five chants, "Accept this my praise, Ganga, Yamuna, Sarasvati, Shutudri (Sutlej), Parushni (Ravi) and Marudhvridha, along with Asikni (Chenab) and Vitasta (Jhelum). Listen Arjikiya with Sushoma."

The next verse continues to chant, "Thou, Sindhu, in order to reach the swift-moving Gomathi (Gumal or

Gomal), hast united thyself first with the Trishtama (now to be united) with the Susartu, the Rasa, the Shweti, the Kubha (Kabul) and Mehatnu in conjunction with which streams thou'st advance." (Translation: Horace Wilson).

Amazingly, this hymn invokes nineteen significant rivers of the Vedic world. Michel Danino, in his book, 'The Lost River,' remarks that "However, of central interest to us, is the hymn's plain statement that the Sarasvati flows between the Yamuna and the Sutlej—precisely the region where British explorers found a wide, dry bed and ruined cities—the region where local traditions assert that a large river flowed once upon a time."

According to Danino, the French geographer, Louis Viviene Saint Martin was the first European scholar (1855) to propose that the Ghaggar river system was a relic of the Vedic Sarasvati. Danino also refers to the Thar desert survey by Lieutenant Colonel James Todd, Major Colvin and Mackeson during the nineteenth century, confirming the truth of Rigvedic chants about the sacred river, Sarasvati.

Even during the twentieth century, H. Wilhemly (geographer), V.M.K. Puri and K. S. Valdiya (geologists in the 1990s), Indologists, such as L. Renou and J. Filliozat (1947), archaeologists, such as Marc Aurel Stein (1917 and 1941), Mortimer Wheeler (1950), R and B Allchin (1982), S.P. Gupta (1989), B.B. Lal (1947), R.S. Bisht (1990s), D.K. Chakrabarti (1990s), Jane Mcintosh (2002) have all accepted apart from others that the Rigvedic Sarasvati was flowing from the Shivalik mountains through Haryana, the Punjab and Rajasthan. Around two thousand BCE, it dwindled and disappeared in a place called Vinashana in the deserts of Rajasthan near the present-day international border. The satellite imagery of the dry Sarasvati river bed is available now along the Ghaggar-Hakra river system due to its high water table. ISRO also confirmed this and published photographs captured by its satellites from above.

Controversies Relating to the River

However, many people are contesting even the existence of the river in the Vedic days. Historian Irfan Habib claims that the river only existed in the imagination of the over-enthusiastic rishis. Another historian, Romila Thapar claims that the Vedic people renamed the Ghaggar river system Sarasvati as a memory of the past. According to her, the original Sarasvati was in modern Afghanistan, and its present name is Hairyavati—in memory of that river, an earlier dwelling point of the Vedic Aryans before invading or migrating further into the Indian subcontinent. Unfortunately, the main agenda of some historians in the opposite camp is safeguarding the much-cherished Aryan invasion theory. Archaeology and Rigvedic texts do not support the Aryan invasion, according to many scholars.

I am a Sarasvat Brahmin. Millions of people like me on the western coast of Maharashtra, Goa, Karnataka and Kerala believe that our ancestors once lived on the banks of the sacred river, Sarasvati and migrated due to adverse weather conditions. Yes, famine is in the community's memory but not an invasion. There is a hilariously comical story about how some Sarasvat Brahmins started eating fish, a delicacy for many of us. During an extended famine, when our people were starving, one of our rishis gave us a special mantra with the help of which fish was cut into three pieces and only the middle piece was eaten. The other two were reconnected, uttering the mantra and were thrown back into the water. Magically, the fish happily swam again—as the legend goes! It is up to you to believe it or take it with a pinch of salt.

Is it an Indus Sarasvati Civilisation?

The archaeologists have located more than two thousand and four hundred sites in the Sarasvati Valley area with definite traces of the Harappan civilisation. With these discoveries, the Sarasvati basin and Gujarat became the central heartlands of the Harappan culture. Therefore, very aptly, S.P. Gupta, an archaeologist of repute, proposed that calling the culture the Indus-Sarasvati civilisation is appropriate instead of the Harappan civilisation. Though some have accepted this proposal, many rejected it. The Pakistanis are at the forefront for apparent reasons.

These ancient sites across the Sarasvati basin prove an archaeological link between the Harappan culture and its spread across northwestern India. These sites also generated very rich finds of artefacts of ancient India. Some of these are used to the day in these areas, confirming the continuity of culture through the ages. The findings also prove that the so-called foreign invaders did not disrupt the Harappan civilisation. The lack of archaeological evidence of the armed struggle in the Harappan sites negates the famous Aryan Invasion Theory. Therefore, modern historians, in their anxiety to enforce their writ when their pet Aryan Invasion Theory seemed to crumble, started proposing the Aryan Migration Theory instead and ultimately settling on the Aryan Trickle-in Theory. Many proponents of the Aryan Invasion Theory now slowly concede that there was no large-scale invasion by the Steppe immigrants. Instead, they are writing about how small bands of migrants trickled in over several centuries.

Many archaeologists have proven that the settlers abandoned the central basin of Sarasvati between 1700 BCE and 1900 BCE due to prolonged famine. The Harappan people also vacated other sites due to extended drought conditions and the disappearance of the mighty Sarasvati, thus further weakening the claim made under the Aryan Invasion Theory.

A few Sarasvats, residing on the river banks of Sarasvati, migrated north towards the Shivalik hills and into Kashmir when the river started drying up. Some went towards the east into 'Gowda Desha' in search of greener pastures. Many migrated towards the south into Saurashtra, Maharashtra and Goa. In his book, 'The Last Prabhu,' my fellow Gowda Sarasvat, Bernardo Elvino de Sousa of Goa, writes about his ancestors' journey from the Sarasvati river basin to Goa after getting his report by the DNA-based genealogy, tracing his family roots for some thirty-six generations. I am quoting this study for scientific reasons. Of course, there are vague ideas about the community's migrations in our memory, based on the Puranic stories (Skanda Purana). Once again, these stories cannot be postulated as the ultimate proof but are indicative of migrations of the Sarasvats to the north, east and towards the Gomantak Coast (Goa) with the accompaniment of a rishi called Parashuram. As per the story, the region of Goa was under seawater. Rishi Parashuram reclaims it with his magical powers to benefit the Sarasvats.

***

6

Other Important Suktas

RV throws many challenges for those who love riddles and enjoy solving them. Here is one such example:

> "Four are his horns, three are the feet that bear him, his heads are two and his hands are seven in number.

> Bound with a triple bond, the steer roars. The mighty God hath entered into mortals (RV 4.58.3)."

> (Translated by Ralph T. H. Griffith)

In the words of Professor Wilson, "It is a good specimen of Vedic vagueness and mystification and of the straits to which commentators are put to extract an intelligible meaning from the text."

Even Sayana offers many interpretations and leaves it to the reader's judgement instead of giving a straightforward commentary to this verse. A fascinating translation refers to this verse as a reminder to all the mortals— "…Kala (death or time) loudly proclaims that He is ever-present in everybody. Why don't you hear the roar?"

However, RV 8.29 has very simple riddles, which are perhaps directed toward the beginners of Vedic learning. The puzzles contained in the fifty-two mantras of RV 1.164 have a difficulty level aimed at senior students. They describe the attributes of deities without naming them, and it is up to the readers to call them correctly.

Women Rishis and Science in the Rigveda

Philosophy is nothing but a love for knowledge in Greek. The same holds good for the Vedic people. The womenfolk were also struck by the love for the truth those days. Therefore, they, too, participated in composing the mantras. The women rishis were also called rishis. The word, rishi was gender neutral. About twenty-one women rishis have contributed to the Rigvedic text. The first recorded reference to the solar eclipse is in the RV, which is the first such mention in any known text worldwide (RV 5.40).

The fifth Mandala is ascribed to a rishi, called Atri. This rishi tells us, "The shadow of a mighty celestial being covers the sun's disc, and it becomes dark everywhere." However, he informs us, "Within a few moments, the shadow moves away, and the sun is bright again." Rishi Atri claims here the credit for finding the sun again with its full glory. The Rigveda also knew that our solar system was heliocentric and not geocentric. The Vedic people knew that the sun was in the centre of other planets rotating around him in the solar system. The Rigveda explores both heliocentric and geocentric ideas of astronomy.

In one of the dialogues between several rishis, one young rishi asks the other (RV 1.35.5-7), "Tell me where the sun goes when it's dark here? Who gets its light?" The wise people of ancient India never thought that the sun's rays were stolen in the evening or that the sun was hiding or something like that, as was believed by some tribes then. They called a full-moon day 'Poornima' (Purna+ma), where 'Purna' is complete, and 'Ma' is the moon. Similarly, they named 'Amavasya' (or A+Ma) a no-moon day, meaning 'a day without the moon.' Their calculations of the day, a year backwards and a year forward, were accurate. How do we know about this? For example, while performing the Ashwamedha Yajna (the horse sacrifice), the finale (or Ahuti) takes place on 'Chaithra Poornima' (the full-moon day of the Chaithra month). Therefore, the preparation must start precisely one year before offering the first oblations. For this, they must know how to calculate the 'Thithis' (days) one year backwards and one year forward without making any mistakes. About eleven-star constellations were mentioned in the RV out of twenty-seven.

What is 'Marimrucha?' It is the thirteenth month (Adhika Masa) or the difference between the Solar calendar and the Lunar calendar, which is adjusted every once in three years. Varsha is nothing but a rainy season. May you live to see a hundred years (Varshas or rainy seasons) is a blessing for youngsters, even today. The text talked about the Saptharshi Mandala (Ursa Major). The rishis named the seven stars in the constellations after the seven important rishis. They even named a tiny star near the star named after Vasista as Arundathi (his wife). To prepare an accurate calendar, they must have known the movements of the moon, the sun and other celestial objects around the globe. How did they calculate this complex set of variables in 2500–3000 BCE without sophisticated gadgets? We do not know.

Animal Sacrifices in the Rigvedic Times

It is common knowledge that in the Ashwamedha yajna, the well-bred horse that went around places to conquer new areas for a year would be ultimately sacrificed. Similarly, in the Soma yajna, they offered a goat.

"They cook for me (for Indra) fifteen plus twenty oxen" (RV 10.84.14).

"Agni is one whose food is the ox and the (barren?) cow" (RV 8.43.11).

Historians believe that the above examples point to the prevalence of animal sacrifices in the Vedic times. But, Vedantic scholars dismiss this claim by saying, "these Pashubalis (animal sacrifices) metaphorically refer to the sacrifice of the animal instincts within us." You can choose your side depending on your liking.

But, as per the Indian National Family Health Survey reports (2020), seventy-eight per cent of the Indian population eats meat. The percentage of meat-eaters is ninety-nine per cent in Japan and hovers around ninety-four per cent to ninety-six per cent in Europe, the US and China. The point to be noted here is that humans grew up eating meat, and we inherited this habit from our ancestors, who were hunter-gatherers. Suppose, the present statistics are used to estimate the percentage of the populace that ate meat during the Vedic period. It may be ninety-eight per cent and upwards, then. In the Pagan era, animal sacrifice was widespread. There is nothing to be surprised if historians' assertions are factual.

Health Science in the Rigveda

Although it is a religious text, the Rigveda gives us an idea regarding diseases, philosophy and management in the ancient world, although in a primitive and mystic manner. This gigantic literature "represented the very best in speculative thinking apart from containing numerous references on drugs, diseases and stars," asserts scholars. It is evident that there were healers for the diseases during the Vedic era:

> The Ṛigveda I.24.9.

> "Oh, King, hundreds, nay, thousands are your healers. (Then why are you suffering so?)"

In this period of magico-religious medicine, the diseases were largely considered to be either the wrath of various Gods and supernatural powers or harmful acts of demons. A rich pharmacopoeia widely spread in the Vedic literature is quite significant. Various sages, such as Angirasas, Sambu, Jamadagni, Kaṇva and Kasyapa were well known for their expertise in discovering and recognising new herbs for remedial purposes. The mention of tṛidhatu in the Rigveda may indicate a rudimentary beginning of the Tṛidosa Theory—the theory of three major balancing factors of life—Vayu or Vata (air), Pitta (bile) and Kapha (phlegm).

Skincare

We could see people caring for their skin in the Vedic period. The daily application of the perfumes to the skin was very much prevalent:

> "Let these charming dames with noble husbands adorn themselves with fragrant balm and unguent."
>
> RV 10.18.7.

Hairstyling and hair care were also trendy amongst both sexes:

> "There were the white-robed Tṛtsus with braided hair, skilled in song worshipping you with homage and hymn."
>
> RV 7.83.8.

Skin, Hair and Nails, as well as Their Diseases

Amongst the diseases, leprosy, hair diseases, etc., were mentioned repeatedly in the Rigveda: "...ghoṣayai cit pitṛṣade duroṇe patiṃ jūryantyā aśvinau adattam." (RV. I.117.7, 19).

Ghoṣa was healed from her leprosy and could get married by the grace of the divine physicians, the Asvins. A similar incidence comes in the hymn I.117.8, where the physician duo, the Asvins, cured Syava of leprosy.

RV 7.50 gives a picture of a condition that is very much indicative of the guinea worm disease affecting the skin and other body parts:

"An eruption that appears upon the twofold joints, and that which overspreads the ankles and the knees, may the refulgent Agni banish far away— Let not the winding worm touch me and wound my foot."

RV 7.50.2.

The reference to the yellowness of the body or jaundice has been mentioned thus in the text:

"Rising this day, Oh, rich in friends, ascending to the loftier heaven, Surya, remove my heart disease—take from me this my yellow hue." (RV I.50.12). Even modern allopathic doctors suggest sunbathing for the cure of jaundice.

Hair disorders have also found a place in RV; Verse 126.7 of Book One perhaps was an example of hypertrichosis—a condition considered an annoying feature in a woman during this period. On the contrary, the menfolk considered light hair a disease. Remember Rishi Apala, about whom we discussed earlier, who asked for hair growth on her father's head?

A few more examples are:

"From what is voided from within,
and from thy hair, and thy nails,
From all thyself from top to toe,
I drive thy malady away."

(ṚV10.163.5.)

"From every member, every hair disease
that comes in every joint,
From all thyself, from top to toe,
I drive thy malady away."

(ṚV 10.163.6.)

Management of Skin Diseases

In Vedic medicine, the management strategy of diseases was composed of a complicated method of chanting mantras, offering oblations and performing some intricate rituals. Along with these, herbs, organic and inorganic materials, as well as procedures, such as anointments, water therapy, etc., are used liberally. The physicians were required to know about the medicinal properties of plants:

"He who hath store of herbs at hand like kings
amidst a crowd of men—Physician is that sage's
name—a fiend-slayer, a chaser of disease."

(ṚV 10.97.6.)

Anointment was a standard method of therapeutic measure practised by the Vedic physician. It is evident from Hymn 10.161 that the physician recited the mantra and touched the various parts of the diseased body with his hands which were anointed with ritually prepared clarified butter (ghee).

In verse 7.50.2, the description suggests burning decayed tissues with fire.

Verses 50.11–13 of Book One suggest knowledge of heliotherapy, particularly in treating the yellowness of the body.

The Vedic seers also used water for the management of various diseases (Hydrotherapy of modern Naturopathy?):

"Amrita is in the waters. In the water, there is a healing balm. Be swift, ye Gods to praise them." (ṚV I.23.19.)

"Within the water—Soma thus hath told me— dwell all balms that heal, and Agni, he who blesseth all. The water holds all medicines."

(ṚV I.23.20.)

Vedic physicians also used their tender touch for remedial purposes. It was, of course, not very clear if it was a type of massage therapy or part of hypnotherapy or touch therapy (as is used these days in the alternative system of medicine—Reiki?)

"Felicitous is this mine hand, yet more felicitous is this. This hand contains all healing balms, making whole with a gentle touch."

(ṚV 10.60.12.)

The rejuvenation of the aged, as in the case of sage Cyavana (ṚV I.116.10, 117.13, 5.74. 7.71.5, RV 10.39.4, etc.) and that of sage Kali (ṚV I.112.15; 10.39.8) was a fascinating description of an aesthetic approach toward the ageing skin and its ailments during the Vedic era.

Unthyesti Yajna Sukta

You have offered many oblations to Agni during your life. When you are dead, you give your body to the fire God, as you are not left with anything else.

"Don't burn him through, Agni. Don't scorch him or singe his skin or body.

When you make him cooked to readiness, Jatavedas, then deliver him to the forefathers.

Then, he embarks on the (way) leading to (the other) life. He will follow the Gods' will.

Let your eye go to the sun, your life breath to the wind. Go to heaven and earth as is fitting.

Or go to the waters, if it has been fixed for you there. Take your stand in the plants with your limbs." (RV 10.16)

After the cremation of the body, the early Vedic people used to bury the remaining bones of the dead by putting them in an earthen jar. During the last rites, the Rigvedic mantra chanted, "Oh, Mother Earth, take the deceased into your custody and keep him always guarded under your wraps of clothing, like a child."

The Last Mantra

The first mantra of the last hymn (one hundred and ninety-one) of the tenth mandala lauds Agni. Later, the hymn prays for material wealth for the community. But in the final mantras, the rishi wishes that the people meet and talk to each other lovingly. He adds, "Let there be a commonality in thought, commonality of action, as well as like-mindedness and equality of all in the tribe."

That, perhaps, is the first clue of socialist thought. Or humanity would not have come this far without these great thoughts. All the tribes of the ancient world propagated these sentiments in their unique way.

Whether we understand the epic text in its proper perspective or not, the narrative makes us read it repeatedly. Some mantras have become a part of Indian worship and rituals, even today. From that point of view, we need to devote some time and attention to the text.

The Vedic Inclusion

Aspirations of the Vedic Commoner

In the Rigveda (9.112.3), a curious mantra says, "My father is a physician and my mother grinds (corn) with stones. I am a singer (reciter of hymns). We desire to obtain wealth in various actions because we live like cattle (in a shed) in this world."

A couple of stanzas earlier, Rishi Shishu of the Angiras family laments, "Various are the occupations of the men (and their wishes). A carpenter desires timber, a physician wishes disease. The Brahmana likes the flow of Soma."

There was a perfect understanding of the dignity of labour amongst Vedic people.

At the same time, no strict hierarchy was noticeable in society during the early Vedic period. In the Rigveda (Hymn number 3.44–45), the rishi prays to Indra— "Hey, Indra, who loves Soma, make me the protector of people or make me a king, or a sage who drinks Soma. You may give me lots of wealth instead."

This chant suggests that the rishi was okay with any role in society.

The Origins of Some Words in the Rigveda: Manusha

The word 'Manusha' appears in all the Indian languages with variations. But it usually means 'the human being.' But this word had entirely different connotations in the Vedic period.

Interestingly, even the Vedic civilisation had its version of the flood story, like the early Sumerians (the story of Gilgamesh) and Noah's episode in the Old Testament of the Bible. In those narratives, God instructs a hero to construct a boat to escape the imminent floods. In Indian mythology, 'Manu' was that hero who got the tip from heaven above. He clears away with God's help (in the form of a fish—Matsyavatar) with his family members and seven wise men. He thus becomes the ancestor of all human beings living today in the subcontinent. Manusha, as per the Vedic Sanskrit, denotes those who came from Manu. It is a symbolic reference to Manu and was eventually used as the common noun for humans. The word reflects a similar meaning in many Indian languages of the day.

Purusha

Similarly, 'Purusha' was used in the Rigveda to denote the gender-neutral 'Cosmic Being' (Purusha Sukta: Tenth hymn of the tenth Mandala). In this hymn, Purusha is a being with a thousand heads, eyes and legs enveloping the entire Universe and extending beyond ten fingers' length. Later, the concept does lead to an interaction between the Purusha force and Prakriti (nature). This interplay leads to all the living and non-living things in this Universe. The fact that the self-sacrifice of this Cosmic Being leads to all creation is another interpretation. Many alternative narratives make the Rigveda fascinating while proving its openness to various ideas. Hundreds of wise men contributed to the core of the Vedas, and the Vedic civilisation accepted alternative narratives with excitement. The conflicting concepts appear in the text very naturally. Therefore, the Vedas stand out as unique in all the world's scriptures. The word 'Purusha,' later became a synonym for a human as the origin of all creations was that Universal Being called Purusha.

Meanings of Dasa and Dasyu

There is considerable controversy amongst historians about these terms. Some Indian and Western historians claim that 'Dasa' and 'Dasyus' refer to apartheid. But nobody has fully understood the Vedic language so far, which is apparent from the different meanings attributed to the same mantras. These words may also refer to non-believers (in fire rituals), demons or barbarians. The Rigveda (10.22.8) describes Dasyus as 'savages' who have no laws, different observances, a-Karman (who do not perform rites) and who act against a person without knowing the person. During that period, the world over, people called their foes 'savages' or 'barbarians.' It does not mean that it was an act of apartheid as practised by the medieval civilised world.

In the entire text of the RV, the word 'Anasa' occurs only once used by 'Aryas,' referring to Dasas/Dasyus. A few historians have translated that word as 'flat-nosed.' They have conveniently used this word to suggest the war between the 'Aryans' and aboriginal Indian early settlers. But if one reads Sayana's commentary on the RV, he breaks the word 'Un-Asa' and informs us that it can also mean 'mouthless.' It does not mean that the Dasas were mouthless, but it indicated that they could not utter mantras properly or speak the language correctly. The Anaryas (non-Aryans) were 'Mridhra-Vacha' (unclear, soft, hostile, scornful or abusive).

Few have also propagated a theory that the dark people mentioned in the RV were Dravidians forced to migrate to the southern part of the country by the Aryans. But T. R. Shesha Iyengar asserts, "In the oldest extant Tamil classics, no traditions point to a home outside the Tamilakam (Tamil land)."

On the contrary, these texts are replete with praises of Vedic Gods, the Vedas, the Vedic hymns, sacrifices, fire rituals, etc.

Similarly, K. A. Nilakanta Sastry states, "There does not exist a single line of Tamil literature written before the Tamils came into contact with, and let us add, accepted with genuine appreciation, the Indo-Aryan culture of North Indian origin."

Michel Danino also agrees with these assertions when he states that "the Dravidian culture has accepted the Vedic culture with its own variety."

American historian and Indologist, H. H. Hock supported the Aryan Invasion Theory, but he stated (2005), "The terms 'black' or 'dark' are referring to the dark world of the Dasas/Dasyus in contrast to the world full of lights of the Aryans—the contrast between the good and evil/dark forces that pervade the Vedas and has many parallels in the world of mythology and scripture of other cultures."

Some Interesting Aspects of Rishis

Though we hear many stories about the Vasistas and the Vishwamitras of the Rigvedic period, they were not the dominant rishis. The Angirasas and the Bhrigus played vital roles in composing the Rigveda. The rishis from the Angiras family have two whole Mandalas (number Four and Six) exclusively. Other families did not have this honour. Therefore, they were equal to the God, Agni in many verses of the RV (1.1.6; 31.1; 31.2; 4.3.15; 9.7; 5.8.4; 10.7; 6.2.10; 11.3). They were also praised as Indra (1.100.4; 130.3), the Asvins (1.112.8) and Ushas (7.75.1; 79.3).

The Bhrigus did not have a family Mandala, though they introduced fire rituals and Soma offerings in the yajnas. They were viewed with scepticism in the early Vedic period because of their earlier association with the Anus. The Bhrigus appear as the enemies of Sudas in the RV 7.18.6. However, in the later RV, the Bhrigus are equated with Angirasas. They played a crucial role in composing four non-family Mandalas (1, 10, 8 and 9). Suktankar of Bhandarkar's Oriental Research Institute, Pune, has conclusively proved that the descendants of the Bhrigus were responsible for the final structure of the Mahabharata epic as we know it today.

Jamadagni is an ancestor of the Bhrigus and was half Bharatha-Puru from his mother's side. He was a nephew of Vishwamithra and had a close association with Angirasas. These associations are a pointer to how Rigvedic Aryans were a close-knit family.

Danastutis (Gift Praises)

The 'poet-rishis' of the Rigveda were generous in praising the kings and princes for the donations from these patrons for the ritualistic services rendered. These verses praising the donors are called the 'Danastutis.' They may have served multiple purposes. The verses pleased the giver of 'Dana' (gift) for sure. At the same time, they spread the message about the importance of the particular rishi who received the gifts. It might have also served as a gentle reminder to the other donors about the stature of the rishi, hinting at what kind of 'Dakshina' the priest deserved.

The cattle were coveted and the most sought-after wealth in those days. Rishi Babru of the Atri clan proudly declared that King Rinchayana of the Rusamas gave him four thousand cows as a gift for the yajna he conducted (the RV 5.30.12-15). He rejoiced when the generous king had given him even the metal jug/pot covered with gold.

Rishis also loved horses, especially when gifted by kings. In RV 5.33.8–10, Samvaran Prajapatya (a rishi from the Vishwamitra clan, included in the family book of Atris) elaborately mentions gifts from the renowned king Trasadasyu. He gives him ten horses, but it comes first, and later, he records a gift of a thousand horses from another king. He records even the colours of horses donated and the unique attributes lovingly.

Donations Given to Rishis

Similarly, in another verse, there is a mention of two dark red horses and three hundred cows received in gifts. In RV 8.5.37, Brahmathiti from the Kanva clan chants about a hundred camels and a thousand cows received from King Kashu, the son of Chedi.

But the most liberal praise was reserved for King Prithushravas, son of Kanita (the RV 8.46.22-31), by the rishi named Vasha, son of Ashva. In these ten verses, he chants, "I have received ten thousand horses, hundreds of camels, a thousand brown mares and three times ten thousand cows with three red patches." It narrates many such tall claims, records a gift received from an enslaved person, Balabrutha, a cowherd and ends with a tall maiden decked in gifted gold jewellery given to him. You will wonder what kind of banter this is after reading these verses.

However, the praises of donors are secondary. The first and foremost is eulogising the deities (such as Indra, Varuna, Vayu, the Maruts and Soma) of the hymns praying for showering good fortune on them.

Nature and the Rigveda

The Vedic people knew the importance of nature, the environment and other living beings. Therefore, rishis created verses praising them and made it a point to create many rituals around them. People worshipped their animals and prayed for the well-being of all the quadrupeds (four-legged ones). Their prayer was always for the thousand-branched tree to spread across the Universe (RV 3.8.11, 9.5.10). Rishis declared, "Do not cut trees because they remove pollution." (RV 6.48.17)

The 'earth' and 'heaven' are addressed as a single being (Dyavaprithvi) and praised. They are 'parents of the Gods' (RV 7.53), and the hymn claims their wealth is unlimited and they protect it. The Sukta declares them as 'father and mother' of all living beings, invoking their blessings for the immortality of progeny (RV 1.159). Together, they keep all creatures safe (RV 1.160). "Heaven is my father. My mother is this vast earth, and both have blessed our daughters' womb with fruitfulness." (1.164.33)

The worship of cattle, mountains, rivers and forests symbolised the Vedic era's importance of nature and the surroundings.

Agriculture in the Rigveda (RV 4.57)

Vedic people wished cattle to give sweet milk by eating great grass grown in the blessed lands. All agricultural implements are worth worshipping for them. Ploughs, ploughshare, hoes, sickles and 'Parjanya' (rain God) have been praised for bountiful crops. Some hymns have been dedicated to the levelling of fields and cultivation and the desire for fertile fields (Urvara), producing rich harvests after rains. Similar practices can be seen in the modern days too.

However, agriculture was a secondary activity during the Vedic period, and domestication of animals was the priority job. Because the hymn under discussion begins with the herds of cattle giving sweet milk. Some hymns refer to conflicts amongst Vedic people to protect sons, grandsons, cattle, watercourses and fertile fields. Therefore, rishis always prayed for many sons to defend the family property and undertake labour-intensive agricultural activities.

Hymn number 5.83 is primarily devoted to bringing out the importance and contribution of the rain God (Parjanya) in raising the fertility and nutrients of the soil. At the same time, the devastating effects of the Maruts (storm Gods) accompanied by the rains are vividly narrated in this Sukta. We chant this hymn even in modern times to invoke rain Gods when rain becomes deficient.

Various Other Activities of the Vedic People

Many hymns of the RV refer to cattle-rearers, farmers, hunters, barbers and some stanzas mention chariot-making, cart-making, carpentry, metalworking, tanning, sewing, weaving and making mats out of grass or reeds. However, there are only a few mentions of metallurgical activity. The word, 'Ayas' (steel) appears in the Rigveda to describe Indra's thunderbolt and columns of the chariot of Mitra and Varuna. A hymn to Agni prays for 'a fort of Ayas.' Ayas could have meant copper, copper-bronze or a generic term for metals. Who knows?

Soma, the drink, was reserved for the elite. For the general public, Sura was enough. This intoxicant drink was made out of fermented grain. The people wore cotton and woollen cloth and animal skin with various ornaments. Singing and dancing were their passions, and chariot racing and gambling were popular. People who did not respect Vedic Gods were called A-Vrata, and those who did not offer sacrifices to fire gods were A-Kratu.

***

7

Battles in the Rigveda

Rigveda Samhita (6.75) devotes a full Sukta to help the royal priest (Purohita) bless the warriors and the chieftain on a military expedition.

The hymn invokes deities to bless the armour, bows and bow tips, the quiver holding the arrows, the chariots and reins and horses in an elaborate and flowery language to protect the soldiers and destroy the enemies.

They do not forget Soma and chant, "(Hey you there!) Let Soma shower blessings on you to make your body like a stone and let Soma dress you up in ambrosia." Our ancestors believed that the drink, Soma had special powers to fortify the soldiers from enemy attacks and multiply their fighting skills.

Defence experts say that half the battle is won in the minds of the soldiers before winning it on the battlefield. The Vedic people knew this aspect well. How else could they have inspired or encouraged the frontline soldiers to give their best? The priests told them they were invincible and their arms and armours were impregnable. It is psychological warfare to boost the army's morale, and it profoundly impacts the soldiers.

Dasarajna Battle (The Battle of Ten Kings)

Three Rigvedic hymns (Mandala 7.18, 33 and 83) describe the battle. Scholars from both sides of the divide agree that this battle is historically significant as it depicts a real account. But as usual, the Vasistas, the composers of Mandala Number Seven, were frugal with the details. They had composed many mantras in these hymns to drum up their contribution to the victory of Sudas, the Puru King.

However, we get the names of different active tribes during the Rigvedic period from the hymns and hints about what happened to them. The confederation of ten tribes fought on the banks of river Parushni (Present-day Ravi) against King Sudas. The sacred text records the names of ten generations of this Puru/Bharata King. There are verses dedicated to the rishis who composed the text's mantras over centuries. Other than them, the Purus/Bharatas share this kind of honour in the Rigveda.

According to R. N. Dandekar, an Indologist and Vedic scholar connected to Bhandarkar's Oriental Research Institute, Pune, 'Puru,' 'Anu,' 'Yadu,' 'Turvasa' and 'Druhyu' were five clans or the 'Panch Janaha.' These five communities followed the Vedic lifestyle. Sudas, a very ambitious and great warrior, wanted to bring the Panch Janaha and other non-Vedic communities under his control and command.

Because of the difference of opinion, King Sudas brushed aside Vishwamitra and anointed Vasista as his chief priest. Infuriated by that, Vishwamitra walked to other Panch Janahas to warn them about the intentions of Sudas. Dandekar believed many skirmishes occurred between the parties earlier, leading to the main confrontation on the river Parushni.

As per Professor H. D. Velankar's observation, "We do not get any important information about the actual fight between the two parties but only the frustration of the attempts of the powerful enemies to overpower Sudas and his Bharatas." (Introduction to the Rigveda Seventh Mandala)

Velankar believes that the culmination of war results from the Ashwamedha yajna conducted by King Sudas—by defeating all the adjacent kings and chieftains in the year-long run of the sacrificial horse around the area.

Michael Witzel claims that (from 'The Indo-Aryans of Ancient Southeast Asia') "...The entire Book number Seven is a snapshot of history—the incursion of Bharata into the Punjab from across the Sindu and their battle with the 'Five People' and Puru. It celebrates the victory of Sudas in the 'battle of ten kings,' which—once and for all—established the supremacy of the Bharatas in

Punjab and set the stage for the formation of the first South Asian state under the 'Kuru' tribe."

He also records that the battle took place near 'Manusha,' a location "that was in the west of Kurukshetra and was won by breaking the natural dyke by the Bharatas. Their eventual arrival on the Yamuna and the defeat of the local chief, Bheda are finally chronicled in 7.18.19."

We can go through some of the verses relating to the war.

(RV 7.18.5ab)

"Indra made even vast flowing waters shallow (of Parushni) and easily fordable to Sudas." (Translation: Valenkar)

(RV 7.18.7ab)

"The Pakthas, the Balinas, the Alinas, the Visanins and the Sivas did loudly sing (their 'Nivids' to Indra)" (Translation: Valenkar)

(RV 7.18.19)

"The Yamuna and the Tristus pleased Indra. Here, did he plunder Bheda thoroughly. The Ajas, Sigrus and the Yaksus brought him their tributes— namely, the heads of the horses." (Translation: Velankar)

(RV 7.18.11)

> "King Sudas cut his foes—like a skilful (priest) who cuts down the grass to prepare a seat—when he overthrew twenty and one tribes of the two Vaikarnas with a desire for fame. Brave Indra arranged for their quick despatch." (Translation: Velankar)

(RV 7.18.15)

These Tristus' executed their task by backing Indra—swooping down upon the enemy like the water moving downwards upon being released (by Indra after killing Vritra). The enemies who had terrible friends abandoned all their possessions to Sudas even though they were careful measurers knowing even the tiniest fraction. (Velankar)

(RV 7.33.3cd)

> "Thus indeed did Indra save Sudas in the Dasarajna war, owing to your hymns, oh Vasistas." (Velankar)

(RV 7.33.5)

> "Being surrounded and distressed in the Dasarajna war, they prayed to Indra as the thirsty men looked up to the heavens (for rains). Indra heard while Vasista was praising him and gave ample freedom to Tristus." (Velankar)

(RV 7.83.4)

"You have protected Sudas, oh Indra and Varuna, subjugating Bheda with your deadly weapons in an inimitable manner. You had heard the hymns of these (Tristus) when they called for help. The priestly service of Tristus became effective."

(RV 7.83.8ab)

"You gave help to Sudas, who was surrounded in the Dasarajna war, oh Indra and Varuna." (Translation: Velankar)

Importance of the Rigveda's Dasarajna Battle

As per Shrikant Talageri, Bharata Purus lived in Kurukshetra to begin with. They were a sub-tribe of Purus. The Bharata Puru wars have been fought through many generations of Bharata's clan. The kings from this clan included Devavata, Srinjaya, Deodasa, Sudas, Sahadeva and Somaka. They all appear in the text many times.

Many generations separated King Sudas from his earlier kings and later kings. The older books Six, Three, Seven, Four and Two belong to Bharata Purus. After that, book numbers One, Five, Eight, Nine and Ten refer to the Purus in general, whose ancestors were Bharata Purus of old books. Srinjaya was the father of Deodasa and Sahadeva was the father of Somaka. The relationships are clear from the text. It is challenging to prove any other relationship between other protagonists of the text. Talageri claims all others have generations dividing them.

RV describes many battles in its text. But the details are so minuscule that it is difficult to distinguish anything from the mentions. However, the three wars under Srinjaya, Sudas, Sahadeva and Somaka are critical from a historical perspective. These wars ultimately led to the emigration of the last four branches (Iranian, Armenian, Greek and Albanian) of Indo-European (Aryan) languages from their original Proto-Indo-European homeland, which was in North India, claims Talageri.

We must remember that forty-six per cent of the world's population speaks Indo-European languages as a first language. RV provides the only recorded evidence of the migration of Indo-European languages from the homeland. These migrations took place after the earlier five departures. With the departure of the last four branches from their land, only one unit of the Indo-European language remained in India out of twelve components. The unit that stayed in India won three wars as was described in the RV. The winners were none other than the Bharata-Purus.

According to Talageri, Iranians, Armenians, Greeks and Albanians were represented by the Anus. Three crucial battles were:

* Hariyupiya battle, fought by Srinjaya in Haryana.
* The Battle of Ten Kings, fought by Sudas and others, was the most vital war that he fought in Pakistan's part of the Punjab.

✳ The Varsagriha battle that Sahadeva and Somaka fought in Afghanistan.

These battles show how the Anus (proto-Iranians) moved westwards and ultimately out of India. Interestingly, the Anus were the allies of Bharata Puru in the first battle against their southern adversaries.

Talageri categorically states that the RV is not the ancestral text of the people of the Indian subcontinent. The old Mandalas, Six, Three, Seven, Four and Two specifically pertain to Bharata Puru sub-tribes. The latest Mandalas refer to the Purus in general. Bharata Purus lived in Haryana, and other Purus lived in present-day UP's western and central parts. These parts of the Indian subcontinent were called 'Bharatha Varsha' initially and because of this name, our country came to be known as Bharath, thanks to Bharatha Purus. We must remember that the Purus were one of the Indo-European tribal conglomerates. The other branches (eleven) migrated out of India.

There were other branches to the east and south. The Yadus dominated the parts of the south of Haryana. At the same time, Turvasus populated the southeast of Haryana, and Ikshwakus were in the east, up to Bihar. The Anus were in the majority in the north and northwest, and the Druhyus used to stay in Western Punjab. And at that time, the Purus in Haryana were sandwiched bang in the middle. Though all these tribes spoke the Indo-European language, they were non-Vedic and were considered non-Aryans by the Purus. In later years, the Vedic culture spread to other areas slowly as the people following the RV started adopting the local beliefs and mythology. This ultimately became part and parcel of Hinduism as we know it today.

The first battle described in the RV (6.27) occurred during Srinjaya's (Deodasa's father) reign on rivers Hariyupiya and Yayavathi (tributaries of Sarasvati). In this war, the Turvasus and the Yadus invaded Haryana and fought against the combined forces of the Purus and the Anus. The Purus emerged victorious with the help of the Anus, who later became their adversaries. A Parthava King, Abayavartin Cayamana, headed the Anus at that time. There is a mention of Lake Manusha of Haryana in certain hymns. Avesta has a recorded history and remembers many details of the battles.

Book Three (the Vishwamitras), hymn thirty-three, describes Sudas crossing over rivers Vipas and Saturdi to expand westwards. Hymn fifty-three talks about Vishvamitra conducting the yajna for Sudas and releasing the horse for conquests in all four directions (Ashvamedha) to gain riches. No other details are available after that in the hymn. Maybe Sudas did not achieve the results as was desired. Was this the reason for Vishvamitra's ouster and Vasista taking over as the principal priest of the Purus? The text is silent on this aspect.

The above hymn does not talk about any other battle. Verse thirty-three records that Vishvamitra chanted mantras to calm the rivers while crossing them. Talageri feels that the Sudas travelled westwards searching for Soma, which was in short supply.

Hymns Eighteen, Thirty-three and Eighty-three of Book Seven deal with the Dasarajna war. Supplementary information is available in hymns Five, Six and Nineteen. Hymns Eighteen to Twenty refer to a battle on the banks of the Yamuna, and the names of the adversaries mentioned there sound very Vedic. Bheda, Ajas, Sikru, Manyamana, Yaksus, Devaka, Turvasa and Matsa sound similar to the present-day Indian names. There is a mention of the Purus in Hymn Thirteen, which must refer to the non-Bharata Purus. While looking at the names of the opponents of the Sudas, they all disappeared from Indian memory later, except for one—the Bhrigus. The Bhrigus joined hands with the Purus later and were given the demi-god's exalted position in the later RV. The opponents, such as Prathu/ Parthavas, Parsus/Parsavas, Simyus, Druhyus, Balanas, Kavi Cayamana, Alinas, Pakthas, Sivas, Vaikarnas, Visanins, Kavasa, etc., appear more in the names of Iranians, Armenians, Albanians, Greek tribes and in the records of Avesta.

The westward departure of the opponents is described in verses numbered 7.5.3 and 7.6.3. According to Talageri, the Alinas of the RV became Hellene in Greek tribes later. The Phryge/Phrygians of Turkey were a branch of Bhrigus of the RV, and the Dacians of Romania and Bulgaria were the Dasas. Sirmione/ Sirmium of Albania were Simyus. Avesta's Kaos was Kavasa, and Kauui was Kavi. These tribes became the ancestors of the Iranians. Later, they also contributed to Croatia, Bulgaria and other Eastern and Western European countries.

Witzel accepts that Balana refers to Baluchis and Paktha as Pakthoons. These tribes were mentioned only in two hymns and six verses of the RV. It is a fascinating story of the movement of humanity and their intermingling. The Varsagira battle was the last of the Bharata Puru wars described in 1.100 (elaborates protection of Indra with the Maruts available to fire-worshippers), 4.15 (describes Sahadeva and Somaka) and 4.30 (describes many battles fought by Indra for the benefit of the Purus). A series of wars had been fought in Afghanistan to evict Bharata Purus's enemies finally. The heroes of these wars were Sahadeva and Somaka. These battles also find a place in Avesta. In Hymn 1.100.17, a few other heroes are mentioned. They are Rajrasva, Suradasa, Ambarisa and Bhayamana. In the following hymn, Arna and Citraratha are recorded as 'Aryas' (i.e. Bharata Puru) who fought on the enemy side. Another hero who fought on the Iranian side was Manuscitra, as per Iranian records, a descendant of Manu.

The Iranian texts recorded the names of Rajrasva and Sahadeva, though their names have been modified to suit them(Arejetasva and Hushdiv). In Book Six (the oldest book), the leader of the Anu coalition (proto-Iranian) was Abhayavartin Cayaman. In Book Seven, the leader of the enemy confederate was Kavi Cayamana. The Avesta refers to their royal dynasty as

Kauuii's dynasty (descendants of Kavi Cayamana) in Afghanistan. Parthians inherited this kingdom in later years.

Talageri claims that the Anatolian (Hittite) and Tocharian branches were the first to emigrate. Five Western European tribes followed them, and they were: Italic, Celtic, Germanic, Baltic and Slavic. Finally, five branches were left in the Homeland (India): Albanian, Greek, Armenian/Thraco Phrygian, Iranians and Indo-Aryan (Vedic) —the order in which the twelve branches migrated from their homeland— wherever it is. The Punjab and Afghanistan area's battles resulted in the third great migration of the last four branches (Anus): Albanian, Greek, Armenian, and Iranian.

The present-day priests of Jews are called Atharvans (the Bhrigus). The Bhrigus were priests of the Anus, and each tribe had its high priest. The priests of Druhyus, the Celtic Druids, were called Dhrui. These priests are remembered in Avesta. The Bhrigu/Atharvans are recorded as the enemies of Zarathustra in Avesta.

The Bharatha Purus gained prominence after these wars. Slowly, the Vedic culture merged with the Nature worship of the Yadus, the Tantric culture of the east, the Philosophical thinking of Ikshvaku and Idol/temple worship of Central and South India to emerge as the Hinduism we know today.

The Power of Mantras

The Vasistas claimed that their constant chanting of mantras in praise of Indra and the oblations they offered to him was why Sudas triumphed in the battle(Dasarajna war). They asserted that Sudas was almost isolated and was on the verge of defeat at a crucial moment in the war. In the hymn, they then tell us that magical Indra and the clan members of the Vasistas appeared on the scene to help Sudas out. Indra starts slaying the enemies with the Beda clan's head, who supported the confederation.

Varuna, the rain God, helps Sudas in the battle by creating shallow waters for his free movements. Varuna also blocks the enemy soldiers by restricting their free movements—by raising water levels on their side of the battlefield. The rishis also hail Mitra with Varuna for the help rendered in the battle and credit Tristus (Puru clan) for the victory.

The Importance of the Battle for Historians:

The historians are sure that the ten kings fought their battle on the river, Ravi, a tributary of the mighty Sindhu River of greater Punjab. Unfortunately, the text gives only a little information. The hymns do not talk about the places of origin of each tribe. They also do not divulge any information about the place from where King Sudas brought his army to fight the enemy confederation. The hymns do not reveal who the attacker was and who was defending. What was the reason for this great battle?

How many troops participated? All these crucial details are missing in the narratives.

The verses state that six thousand six hundred sixty-six soldiers died in the war and gave full credit to Indra and his magical powers. The hymns also praise the help received from Mitra and Varuna. The distinction is unabashedly given to the impact of the chantings of the Vasistas. The verses commend King Sudas for his bravery and equate him with Indra, with some reluctance. If the text had given more details, the entire debate about the historical aspects might have ended. The editor, Shakala, must have chopped off many verses written on the issue while editing. We could not lay our hands on Bhashkala's edition of the RV, which we are told was elaborate. We can only pray to mighty Agni to discover his edition one day. It is also possible that his detractors threw Bhashkala's edition into Agni.

War and Peace Initiatives of the Vedic Period

The Rigvedic verses inform us that six thousand six hundred sixty-six died in the Dasarajna war. But does not tell us how many were injured and maimed for life. It must have far exceeded the fatalities sustained in the war initiatives. Ten million was the population estimate of the Indian subcontinent (including present-day Pakistan, Bangladesh and Nepal) during the Vedic times. The Sindhu basin area must have had a population of a million at the most during that period. Roughly, not more than about fifty thousand people must have participated in the battle. Even if thirty per cent of the soldiers died or got wounded for life, it would have been a significant trauma for them.

In addition, the Vedic people must have been aware of what happened in the faraway cities of Mesopotamia. In that area, city dwellers were continuously massacred in the bloody inter-city wars, thus ruining the Sumerian and Akkadian cultures. The wise men were conscious of the cycle of revenge that most wars initiated. Wars did not create anything positive. Death, destruction, trauma and the pain were too much for both sides. The battles must have caused disastrous ill effects on the families of dead and injured soldiers.

But, there were no substitutes for wars during the era. Therefore, they strengthened their negotiation skills to avoid fights. At the same time, they came out with the brilliant idea of voluntarily following a code of conduct during the battles. They mutually agreed on the time to commence and stop indulging in the active fight. They barred the conflicts at night. At that time, there was a clear understanding that the heroes would challenge and fight only his class of adversaries fighting on the other side. Cavalry would fight the cavalry of the other side. No attacks were made from behind—only frontal attacks were allowed. The attack on the civilians was taboo and unheroic.

The epic, The Mahabharata showcases these aspects of controlled fighting without blatant butchering of each other. It was unique for India, and therefore, Megasthenes fumbled when he witnessed farmers going through their agricultural work calmly—when the battle raged in a nearby area. The war always resulted in massacres, rapes and outright killings of innocent people in other parts of the world when lone India fought with a well-drawn code of conduct to reduce the sufferings of the masses.

✳✳✳

8

History and The Rigveda

Scientists inform us that creation started somewhere on the African continent billions of years ago by a freak accident. They tell us that the creative dance of mix and match began in that volatile pool full of cosmic concoctions. They claim that a life form took billions of years of evolution to exist and thrive.

Scientists agree that some ancient single-celled viruses and bacterial life forms may be alive today. However, they claim that the complex creatures on this earth today emanated from the liberal mixing of various life forms. Indeed, blending life forms into typical and varied flora and fauna brings beauty and elegance to planet Earth. The sapiens are no exception to this rule of creation. Anthropologists believe that intermixtures between the various versions of humankind led to the appearance of modern homo sapiens. They claim that the homo sapiens have immensely benefitted from this admixture process. Our precise mental makeup and intense physical attributes directly result from the fusion between different genomes and DNAs. The main reason for the interbreeding of humankind is the constant migration of people worldwide.

Historical Background

Archaeologists tell us that the control of fire by early humans goes back at least one million years. Modern humans (homo sapiens) who lived in caves were adept at handling the fire for cooking, lighting, warmth and protection from wild animals at night. The next significant invention of early humans is said to be 'a wheel.' Sumerian people were credited with this feat which revolutionised the mode of transportation.

Archaeologists also confirm that by 10,000 BCE, inhabitants of the fertile crescent (present-day Iraq and surroundings) knew agriculture to supplement their hunter-gatherer lifestyle. However, upheavals in the environment forced them to move from one place to another in search of food. The benchmark for human civilisation is loosely measured by the extent of urbanisation with monumental buildings supported by organised agriculture with social hierarchy and knowledge of record-keeping.

By 9,000 BCE or earlier, though some places in West Asia had witnessed massive brick constructions, the other conditions were yet to be fulfilled for the emergence of urban centres. Either agriculture was yet to generate the proper food grain surpluses to feed the masses or the hierarchical social setup was not there. Therefore, the population was very sparse. In those days, agricultural activity was a physically demanding profession requiring extended hours of labour. Hunting was far easier for the people because they were adept at it. If the hunting game became scarce, the hunter-gatherers moved to another place. Moving to a different location was out of the question for people solely dependent on agriculture.

The unpredictable and freakish weather conditions we fret about now also troubled the ancient people without mercy. About 8,200 years ago (known as the 8.2 kiloyear event), the world temperature dropped dramatically for one last time. Scientists claim that its effect lasted thousands of years and was acute about six thousand and two hundred years ago. The impact of this climate change rendered the fertile crescent cool and arid. The agriculture in the area suffered severely. The result was that the urban centres disintegrated and dispersed into small bands to other places where the environment was favourable. The smaller groups remained so for the next 3,000 years. Yet, they brought many social and technological developments in their day-to-day lives (the period is also known as Pottery-Neolithic, 6,500-3,500 BCE). The people started using a variety of kiln-fired decorated pottery for storage, cooking, transporting goods, etc. Compared to the earlier plain ceramics, these were more elaborate and painted with animal motifs and geometric patterns.

According to scholars, humans settled permanently in one place at the beginning of the fourth millennium BCE. The frequent changes in weather conditions in the fertile crescent never allowed the people to settle down in one place until then. By 3,300 BCE (the peak of a particular culture), a new civilisation coupled with an urban centre having a population of about fifty thousand people emerged with a temple complex which was well organised along with a specific way of worship, a defined social order and hierarchy.

The city's name was Uruk, which was situated on the river Euphrates' banks, and showed all signs of civilisation, including well-developed agriculture in the hinterlands supporting the city dwellers. The city had marketplaces, meeting places and colossal temple complexes. Basic levels of bureaucratic record-keeping started in this area for the first time. There were two temple complexes in Uruk. One temple in the Eanna district was dedicated to goddess Eanna (who might have been a high priestess, a storekeeper or a princess), and the other was in the older Anu district where the Sun God was worshipped. Priests of the temple were chieftains of the city, who derived their powers directly from the temple Gods—below the Priest-Kings, the keepers, scribes, priests and administrators functioned to maintain the proper order in the city.

The producers, such as farmers and fishers, were at the bottom of the pyramid. A primitive writing system was developed to keep records of taxes, tributes and products. The newer pottery and tools produced there were famous across Syria and Iran. Archaeologists assume that a new kind of pottery wheel emerged during that period. Mass production and the lack of decorative paintings on the pottery made it unique. The civilisation started using cylindrical seals instead of stamp seals to identify and denote authoritative ownership of the goods. However, within the next few centuries, a new organisation system utterly different from the earlier period would emerge in Mesopotamia.

Similar cities on the river basins in the crescent fertile flourished slowly and steadily. The Indian Harappan civilisation was in contact with this region, and much commerce did happen between these cultures. For the people of Sumer, Mesopotamia meant the land between the rivers (Euphrates and Tigris) in present-day Iraq.

Scholars believe that the river banks of Mesopotamia gave rise to the first civilised culture. Unfortunately, the civilisation that flourished in the area vanished without any trace. But it is also true that another civilisation started to thrive on the banks of river Sarasvati almost simultaneously. The Vedic civilisation, which developed on the banks of the once-mighty river, Sarasvati is the only civilisation with an uninterrupted run until the modern era.

Why are the historical aspects of The Rigveda neglected?

It may be unfair for the historians if we brush aside their writings on Vedic people's history. However, their attempts seem to be half-hearted as there are roadblocks. Historians do not have any other archaeological or textual evidence except for the Vedic literature. Historians disdain Vedic literature because of its exaggerated versions containing little factual information.

For a few historians, Vedic literature is the ultimate truth. They believe every word contained in The Vedas. Unfortunately, for those other historians who have reluctantly written on the Vedic civilization, their main focus was on proving or disproving the Aryan Invasion Theory. Another exciting area for them has been discussing whether the Indus Valley civilization was a part of Vedic culture. Despite almost two hundred years of debate, The Rigveda contents never came under the thorough scrutiny of serious historians.

Only a few ventured to study the historical perspective that it can offer. Talageri's book, 'A Historical Analysis of The Rigveda' is a bold attempt in this direction in the recent past.

Historians' Views of The Rigveda

Most historians believe that the contents of The Rigveda have enough material to unravel the historical jigsaw puzzle of the subcontinent. But they feel the archaeological evidence must have precedent over Vedic poetry. Their caution comes from the fact that the earliest surviving manuscript of the text belongs to the 11th century CE.

While many historians believe that The Rigveda Samhita was composed between 1,500–1,000 BCE, others concede that it might have been composed around 2,000 BCE. According to them, Books 2–7 are the oldest, and known as 'family books.' Seer-poets of these books were Gritsmada, Vishvamitra, Vamadeva, Atri, Bharadwaja and Vasishta. In these books, the hymns to Agni come first, then Indra and then the other deities. There is a particular pattern which these family books follow. The arrangement is such that there are fewer verses per hymn in the succeeding hymns than in the preceding Suktas. If there are the same number of mantras in two Suktas, then the hymn in a metre requiring more syllables is placed first. The arrangement of Suktas, other than the 'family books,' follows a different but recognisable pattern.

If there is a disruption in the above order, it could be recognised as an interpolation (Khila Suktas), meaning 'added later.' The scholars could quickly notice the pattern of mixing the old hymns in new books and vice versa. The compilers have made this deliberate and orderly arrangement of the Samhita. The credit must go to Rishi Shakala for the excellent editing work in the Shakala Samhita, the only edition of The Rigveda available to us. The other editions of the text that might have differed are unavailable to us. (For example, Bhashkala Samhita).

Interestingly, a few even used astronomical references in The Rigveda to date the text. For example, Ludwig maintains that the text was composed in the eleventh century BCE. At the same time, Jacobi arrived at the third century BCE timeline. Subhash Kak (2001) believes the text can be dated between 4,000 and 2,000 BCE.

However, the dates earlier than 6,000 BCE, as a few Vedantic scholars claimed, are challenging to believe because archaeology proves that the northwestern part of the Indian subcontinent was in the 'Stone Age.' It is evident from these discussions that the Vedic period or the Vedic culture is subject to many interpretations.

Philologists (scholars who study old languages), linguists, historians, archaeologists and others continuously debate about the original homeland of the Indo-Europeans and Indo-Aryans. The dominant view is that Indo-Aryans came to the subcontinent as immigrants. Some Indian scholars believe that they were of indigenous origin. However, it is an accepted view amongst historians that the original homeland of the Indo-Europeans was in the plains of Eastern Europe (the area north of the Black Sea).

Out of thirty to fifty tribes and clans mentioned in The Rigveda, the five tribes, the Yadus, the Turvashus, the Purus, the Anus and the Druhyus were the main actors. They were collectively called 'Pancha Jana,' 'Pancha-Kristhya' or 'Pancha-Manusha.' The Purus and the Bharatas were the two dominant tribes. The chief of the Purus was Trasadasyu. The Rigveda mentions Divodasa (a famous Bharata king) and describes his victory over the Dasa ruler, Shambara (with many fortresses).

However, it is challenging to distinguish between mythology and history in the text. Many believe that the Dasas and Dasyus were the aboriginal people who fought the new immigrants. In contrast, others insist that these represent the earlier (pre-Vedic) waves of Indo-Aryans who entered the Indian subcontinent. The text also records the enmity between the fellow Aryans. Therefore, it is untrue to state that the battles were only between the Aryans and Dasyus. Overall, the wars were fought to gain territories in human history.

There are plenty of non-Indo-European words in The Rigveda (three hundred words). These words lead to the theory that the Vedic people were in touch with the Dravidian and Munda people. Names, such as Chumuri, Dhuni, Pipru and Shambara indicate this trend. In contrast, the Arya chieftains, such as Balbutha and Bribu had non-Aryan names.

What do historians say?

As per the Puranas, the later commentaries on The Vedas, the ancestor of Vedic Aryans was King Manu Vaivasvata (the Indian flood hero). He had ten sons. But The Puranas talk about only two of them. The first is Ikshwaku, who becomes the originator of the 'Surya Vamshis' or the 'Solar race.' And the second one was Ila, who established the 'Chandra Vamsha' or the 'Lunar race.' Ikshwakus inhabit eastern UP and Bihar.

The Chandra Vamshis (or Ilas) are subdivided into five main tribes: the Purus, the Yadus, the Anus, the Druhyus and the Turvasus. There is a mention of these five tribes in hymn number one hundred and eight of the first Mandala. Where these main tribes first settled is one big contentious issue amongst historians.

If we agree with the order of the Rigvedic Mandalas suggested by Talageri, then the Purus first settled in Haryana and areas of western UP. The Anus lived in Kashmir and to its west. At the same time, the Druhyus started in the Saptha Sindu areas and the Punjab. The Yadus lived in Gujarat, MP and south Rajasthan. Similarly, the Turvasus lived in the east of Yadu area.

The Purus Were the Yajamanas (the Sponsors) of the Vedic Civilisation.

Talageri claims that only Puru areas coincide with the places described in the early books of The Rigveda. There is no doubt that the Purus were the heroes of The Rigveda. Reference to the Puru clan repeatedly appears throughout the hymns of the epic, which proves a point. The river Sarasvati commands three Suktas in the scripture as the river flowed in the Puru areas during Vedic times. They lived on both banks of the river. Western scholar, Michael Witzel agrees with Talageri that The Rigveda belongs to the Puru and Bharata clans.

The Bharatas, the Puru sub-tribes and the Purus are the heroes of the oldest Mandalas (Book numbers Six, Three and Seven). They joined together to fight other branches of the Purus (Non-Bharatas). The Bharata clan even composed and contributed nineteen hymns to The Rigveda. According to many 'Out of India' theorists, when Vedic people called themselves 'Aryas,' it meant only 'Our People.' As per Talageri, the word 'Arya' occurs thirty-four times in the text. About thirty-one times it was used by the Bharatas, the Angirasas, the Vasistas and the Vishwamitras.

Even the rishis belonged to the Puru tribe?

It may be interesting to note that the Angirasas, the Vasistas and the Vishwamitras are the prominent composers of the Rigveda and participated very actively in the war initiatives of the Bharatas. These rishis have conducted yajna rituals to benefit their kings from the Puru and the Bharata clans.

The Rigveda gives details of many such battles in short. In a tribal setup, the group members belonged to the same line. Therefore, it is easy to assume that the wise men belonged to the Puru tribe.

Returning to the second word of the first mantra of Book Number One, 'Purohitam,' apart from its meanings discussed earlier, can also be read as 'for the welfare of the Puru clan.' We tend to ignore other definitions (discussed earlier) of the word after reading Witzel and Talageri's write-up on the connection between The Rigveda and the Purus. Surprisingly, all of us who chant these mantras to this day are the descendants of the Purus!

Mitanni Documents

An inscription found at Bogaz Koi, northeastern Syria (1380 BCE), records a treaty between **Hittite and Mitanni.** It names the Gods, Indara(Indra), Mitras (Mitra), Nasatia (Nasatya, the Asvins), and Uruvanass (Varuna) —the deities of The Rigveda. While local Mitanni people spoke the Hurrian language, the inscription indicates that their rulers had Indo-Aryan names and invoked Aryan Gods. Another Hittite text on horse training and chariotry, written by Kikkuli (a Mitannian), uses many technical terms of Indo-Aryan origin. The archaeologists found the Sanskrit names and phrases in ancient Syria, Iraq and Turkey.

The Mitanni kings ruled this area around 3500 years ago. The names of these kings were Vedic and they used Sanskrit phrases extensively in their treaties. Talageri claims that the Mitanni Kings' ancestors had Vedic antecedents who migrated to central Asia around 3,800 years ago. Therefore, he claims that the Vedic civilisation is over 4,000 years old. The Indus Valley culture was an integral part.

Spoked Wheels

Another alibi Talageri produces is the lack of mention of spoked wheels in the older books of the text. The citation of spoked wheels appears only in the New Books. The usage of spoked wheels commenced in the Indian continent around 2,200 BCE. This fact again pushes back the composition of the early books of the text to pre-Aryan (?) immigration and negates the Western Historians' claims.

But Michael Witzel assumes that the Steppe Aryans first settled in central Asia before moving into Iran and the Indian subcontinent. That premise answers Mitanni's angle and the usage of Sanskrit in their language. At the same time, it strengthens the Western proposition that Sanskrit was brought into India by the Steppe Aryans. But Michael Witzel admits that it needs to be confirmed where the combined Indo-Aryans lived together.

The Spoked Wheel

What do the Zoroastrian scripts indicate?

It is clear from early Iranian text, Avesta that Indo-Iranians lived together in the Saptha Sindu and the Punjab areas. The Avesta discusses the geography of the region. Though Iranians and Aryans worshipped the fire Gods, the Avesta called their God 'Ahura' (Asura) and the demons 'Devas.' The Bhrigus, the prominent rishis of the later Rigveda, used to be the Iranian priests.

The Rigvedic text mentions that the Bhrigus brought Agni, or fire Gods, to the Yajna ritual of the Aryans at the beginning. Despite their critical role, they could get only a secondary role in the composition of the text. Because they were the priests of Iranians or the Anus, the Bhrigus did not get a predominant role initially. In hymn number 18.6 of the seventh Mandala, the Bhrigus appear as enemies of the Sudas, one of the heroes of the text. Later, when the Bhrigus left the Anus (Iranians) and joined hands with the Bharatas, they played a significant role in composing the later parts of the Rigveda.

Contributions of the Bhrigus

Suktankar, in his book, The Bhrigus and the Bharatas, asserts that the Bhrigus have shaped the epic, the Mahabharata as we know it today. Lord Parasurama was a Bhrigu. Their contribution to Hindu Vedantic thoughts was immense. Later, the Bhrigus got a status which was equal to the Angirasas (RV 8.6.18 and 8.43.13).

"Holy Agni, to whom oblations are offered, we worship Thee in a manner worshipped by the Bhrigus, the Manus and the Angirasas," (RV 8.43.143).

The rishis from the Bhrigu 'gotra' added aspects, such as 'Dharma,' 'Artha,' 'Kama' and 'Moksha' to the Indian philosophy. Vatsayana, Kautilya and Shankaracharya were Bhrigus. These events conclusively prove that a significant proportion of Iranian people had been assimilated into the Vedic culture of the Indian subcontinent. Impressed by the contributions made by the Bhrigus, the Rigveda refers to them as Gods in 10.92.10.

Are we all Africans?

The geneticists toured the Kalahari desert extensively and collected blood samples from the most primitive people. These communities still live in isolation in remote areas of the desert without much modern interference. Geneticists studied the DNA structures of the San, Koi and Herer people and the other natives living there. After a careful study, they have drawn some spectacular conclusions.

They confirmed that these people belonged to the species of early humans. But curiously, they inherited distinct 'genomes' and are not closely related. According to the experts, the DNA structures of a modern European and a person from China will closely resemble. But Kalahari bushmen from different areas did not show this kind of affinity. Scientists discovered more and more varieties of 'maternal genomes' from these tribal people.

The harsh conditions in the desert areas must have compelled ancient Africans to move north. The first wave of such migration happened somewhere around

1.8 million years ago. These archaic human species were called 'Homo Erectus.' As per the anthropologists, the second wave of migration must have occurred approximately between 1.4 million and 0.9 million years ago. The third and vital migration happened between 770,000–550,000 years ago.

These movements were crucial because, during this period, modern humans separated from Denisovans and the Neanderthal species of humankind. The Denisovans and Neanderthals again split between 47,000–38,000 years ago. Eventually, they just disappeared from the face of the earth after briefly interbreeding with modern humans, who were migrating out of Africa around 50,000–70,000 years ago.

This journey of modern homo sapiens out of Africa was critical for today's world population. These people are the ancestors of all human beings who inhabit today.

✳✳✳

9

The Aryan Invasion Theory and the Rigveda

When the Archaeologists discovered the aggressive movements of the 'Steppe pastoralists' into the European subcontinent, Central Asia and Eastern Asia, a new theory emerged. New ideas argued that the population of present-day Germany, England and a few other nations had undergone a complete change. The natives of those places vanished into thin air when the Steppe people moved in and attacked them. Therefore, they suggested that India must have gone through the same fate.

However, the text of the RV does not remember anything about the homeland outside India. With their sharp memory, the Vedic Samhita's creators would never have missed such a crucial aspect in their narrative. There is no mention of the Aryans coming from a faraway place in the Rigveda. Many scholars believe that the word 'Arya' suggests that they performed fire rituals propagated by the 'Vedic people' and adhered to their religious norms.

The Speculations of the Historians

The historians did what they were good at when more information was needed. They speculated about the turn of events based on what they claimed as corroborative shreds of evidence. Consequently, Michael Witzel, the proponent of the Aryan Invasion Theory, rearranges the chapters of the Rigvedic Mandalas. He argues that the Mandalas' chronological order based on their antiquity is two, four, eight, five, six, three, seven, nine, one and ten. This rearrangement conclusively proves the movement of Aryans from Western India towards the East of India supporting the Aryan Invasion theorists.

He tells us that his research conclusively proves that the Purus and Bharatas were newcomers to the Indian subcontinent compared to other clans appearing in the Rigveda. Witzel identifies about thirty tribes from the text. He lists the composers' names and identifies the text's geographical features, like rivers and mountains. His writings reflect the political and cultural environment of the Vedic period. By any standards, it is a scholarly work. He concludes his essay by forcefully propagating two politically sensitive points: 1)The Aryan race entered India in the middle of the second millennium BCE. 2) They brought their culture and language into India and defeated native Indians, ultimately resulting in Vedic civilisation.

The Counter-narrative

Shrikant Talageri rebuts Witzel's arguments one by one by pinpointing the errors committed by the latter while putting forward his findings. Talageri complains that Witzel purposefully rearranged the Mandalas' chronology in the Rigveda to prove the Aryan Invasion Theory and questions Witzel's assertion—that it is difficult to know the number of families of rishis involved in composing the text. Talageri tells us that there are ten Apri Suktas. Accordingly, there are ten families of composers. He names the Kanvas, Angirases, the Agastyas, the Gratsmadas, the Vishwamitras, the Atris, the Vasistas, the Kasyapas, the Bharatas and the Bhrigus.

Talageri agrees with Witzel's repeated assertions that Steppe people kept on entering India for a long time. Talageri points out that this is not a big deal at all. Even during the last two thousand five hundred years, many Greeks, Mongols, Turks and Scythians entered the Indian sub-continent in search of wealth. Then, he points out that those who entered India have always assimilated into its culture and traditions. He asserts that it is baseless to claim that the people from the Steppe grasslands have forced their cultural practices and language on the natives.

Out-of-India Theory

Though the Rigvedic text was kept alive through the oral tradition for thousands of years, it has the status of an 'inscription' in the 'archaeological sense.' Only the problem is identifying the correct chronological order of the Mandalas. If we accept the well-researched data from the Rigvedic Mandalas by Talageri, the 'Out-of-India' theory gets a new lease of life.

The oldest book (number Six, as per Talageri) places the Purus of the Rigveda at present-day Haryana, on the banks of the river Sarasvati. Their movement to the northwestern part of India into the Sindu basin area becomes apparent in the later Mandalas. In the Seventh Mandala, which describes the 'battle of ten kings' (7.18; 7.33; 7.83), comes a narration that the losers in the struggle get scattered. "The Anus and a few others who lost the war ran to Iran and slowly moved into present-day areas of Syria, Iraq and Turkey to form the Mitanni Kingdom," Talageri explains. Thus he says, "The Vedic culture and the Sanskrit language spread into the European Continent."

Do Iranians hail from Kashmir?

Talageri argues that the dreamland of early Iranians and one of the sixteen perfect lands discussed in the Avesta by Ahura Mazda was Kashmir. He opines that the Indo-Iranians migrated to the Punjab from Kashmir and later, to present-day Iran. He emphatically states that the original homeland of the Aryans was the state of Haryana. With the help of the narratives from the Rigveda, he tells us that the Aryans moved from the Sarasvati river banks to the Sindu river basin areas. But the only hitch in the argument is that we may have to agree to the chronological order of the Rigvedic Mandalas he postulates. He compellingly argues that the ten Mandalas' correct chronological order is six, three, seven, four, two, five, one, eight, nine and ten. He tells us that the Mandala or Book Number Six of the Rigveda is the oldest, and Book Number Ten is the latest.

Was the Indian subcontinent a dreamland of the ancient world?

Talageri does not negate people's entry from the European grasslands into India. On the other hand, he concurs with the Western scholars that the Steppe people entered India in small numbers over a long period. He tells us that the Huns, the Kushans, the Greeks, the Mongols and hordes of other people entered India during the known period of history. The Indian subcontinent was supposed to be the wealthiest and a comparatively peaceful destination inhabited by friendly people. So it is no big surprise that India lured those ancient pastoralists of the European steppe.

Which is the homeland of Indo-European languages?

According to Talageri, the Eurasian Steppe people entered India in small numbers for a long time, stretching over hundreds of years. They came in silently without violence and intermingled with the natives with the least fuss. Of late, even Western historians agree that there is no archaeological evidence of war during the period. Talageri also puts forward a counter-argument to Michael Witzel's theory that the homeland of the proto-Indo-European language is somewhere in the southern grassland of Eurasia.

Talageri contends that archaic Sanskrit is the mother of all Indo-European languages and gives many examples to prove his version. He points out that the recent 'Genetic Evidence' can confirm only the contribution of the genetic materials by the people who migrated from the grasslands and cannot prove anything about the Steppe immigrants' bringing the Indo-European language and culture into India. Koenraad Elst, a supporter of the 'Out-of-India' Theory, has reviewed Talageri's book and appreciated the efforts put in by him.

Which is the correct chronological order of the Rigvedic Mandalas?

Michael Witzel, the proponent of Western thought, tells us that the chronological order of the Mandalas of the Rigveda is Two, Four, Eight, Five, Six, Three, Nine, One and Ten. He argues that Book number Two is the oldest, and the tenth Mandala is the latest. The Western version of the 'Aryan Invasion Theory (AIT)' gets validated if you agree with him. The Aryan migration from the northwest to the eastern part of the Indian subcontinent emerges from Witzel's Mandalas' order.

The refrain from AIT opponents is that 'the genes don't speak' when Witzel is trying to support the new findings based on 'Genetics.' The dispute has been hogging the limelight for the last two hundred years and cannot be over just yet. Let us leave it to the academicians and scholarly people to fight it out and concentrate on other historical inputs which we can gather from the epic.

Are the Vedic people and Harappans two sides of the same coin?

According to Talageri, the Anus resided in the Sindu river basin area as per the Rigveda. They were a part of the Vedic culture before they lost the war against King Sudas, with Indra's support. B. B. Lal, a famous archaeologist in India, who participated in the excavation work of Harappa and served as the Director General of A.S.I, said that the Vedic people and the Harappans are but two sides of the same coin. We know now that the Harappans were more civilised than the immigrants from the Steppe grasslands.

Many archaeologists have confirmed no traces of battles between migrating Aryans (?) and native Indians of that era. There is evidence of demographic and cultural changes in Russia, Portugal and Ireland. No such proof is available in the Indian subcontinent. Similarly, fire altars were excavated from many Harappan sites, again giving credence to the theory. Furthermore, the Rigveda talks about the fortifications of many chieftains, and the Harappan cities had rock walls around them.

Barbarians in the Civilised World

We are living in a civilised world now. Yet, we have barbarians amongst us! They care little about cultural sensitivities or the majoritarian feelings of humanity. These people 'call a spade a spade' without batting an eyelid. The geneticists are the barbarians of the new era. They can dive into the human history of hundreds of generations and tell us what the genes of modern human beings have in store for us.

In their scholarly paper, 'The Genetic Ancestry of Modern Indus Valley Populations from Northwest India,' submitted in 2018 by geneticists, Ajai K. Pathak and others bring out the aspects of the mixture of populations of the Indian subcontinent.

Their area of interest is the study of the genomes of the ancient Indian population of the northwestern Indian sub-continent, which exists even today in the Indus Valley landscape. They studied the DNA contents of Rors, Jats, Gujjars and Khatris in the area and have given their conclusions. The results of their study are on the expected lines. According to them, Rors, Gujjars, Jats and Khatris have a solid affinity to their steppe ancestry.

DNA flows can unravel a hidden story. Mr. Pathak's and others' paper again confirms that we are distant cousins to Western Europeans! Our forefathers came from Africa. There is no scope for anyone to claim the purity of the descent in this world. Of course, some bushmen from Africa, the Jarawas and the Sentinelese tribe from Little Andamans may fit into the bill to a certain extent! The truth is that repeated breeding between different groups of tribes and races made modern human beings very resilient creatures.

The Aryans are no exception to this rule. That said, Indian women have a unique native mitochondrial DNA, which has been passed by mothers to their daughters. This trend indicates that the Indian lineage from the mother's side has continued for the last five thousand years with the least mix-up.

But the contrarians are asking, "So what? What is the big deal if the genes of the modern Indians match closely with the steppe people? Don't we know that all humans migrated out of Africa and stayed together somewhere in West Asia before relocating to various destinations? Does that not answer why we are all distant cousins?"

The World Was Full of Pagans

As we know, the ancient people were 'pagans.' Whether Egyptian, Roman, Greek, Celt, Indian or Chinese in origin, one's belief system hovered around a set of Gods and demi-gods. And interestingly, the mythological stories belonging to each group of pagans were the mirror image of each other's stories with a bit of a twist here and there. Therefore, it is easy for people from different groups to claim that their story is original and others have copied it. With these fundamental aspects in our minds, let us move on.

Druids—were they the Druhyus who Migrated out of India?

The Druids were the priestly class of the Celtic world of ancient Gaul, Britain and Ireland. They were the spiritual guides and philosophers of the Gauls. Julius Ceasar meticulously kept his war record and made fascinating comments about the people he fought. In one such document, he mentions that the Druids believed "that the soul does not die and that after death, it passes from one body into another. According to their belief, the main object of all education is to imbue their scholars with a firm belief in the indestructibility of the soul, which merely passes at death from one tenement to another. By such doctrine alone, they say, which robs the death of all its terrors, can the highest form of human courage be developed."

In another account, Ceasar writes:

"The Druids officiate at the worship of the Gods, regulate public and private sacrifices and give rulings on all religious questions."

"They act as judges practically in all disputes, whether between tribes or individuals…"

"The Druids are exempt from military service and do not pay taxes like other citizens. These privileges are naturally attractive. Many present themselves on their own accord to become students of Druidism and others are sent by their parents or relatives."

What he states next is very interesting. "It is said that these pupils need to memorise great numbers of verses—so many, that some of them spend twenty years at their studies."

"They also hold long discussions about the heavenly bodies and their movements, the size of the universe and the earth, the physical constitution of the world and the power and properties of the Gods. They instruct young men in all these subjects."

"The Druids believe that their religion forbids them to commit their teachings in writing, although for most other purposes, such as public and private accounts, the Gauls use the Greek Alphabet."

While going through the descriptions of Julius Ceasar, we are reminded of our Vedic rishis. There are many similarities between the Druids, their education system and beliefs and the Vedic culture. Of course, Ceasar exaggerates the fire rituals and their methods of sacrifice by routinely burning live humans during the fire rituals—maybe to impress his audience back in Rome to drive in a point about the kind of barbarians he just conquered.

Finally, he wrote about their favourite gods as follows:

"The god they revered most is Mercury. They have very many images of him and regard him as the inventor of all arts—the god who directs men upon their journey—their most powerful helper in trading and getting money."

This God of the Gauls had goats as his companions, as has been depicted in one of the images. These descriptions remind us of the Vedic God, Pusan, the Sun, which appears on the horizon after the queen of dawn, Ushas.

In the earlier chapter's discussions about the Dasarajna Battle, we have seen that the tribes defeated in the war rebelled against the Vedic belief and started worshipping the 'Asuras' (Ahuras) instead of the 'Devas.' In this context, let us see what Ceasar says about their ideas:

"The Gauls claim all of them descended from their father, Dis (the king of the Underworld), thus declaring that it is the tradition preserved by the Druids. For this reason, they measure time not by days but by nights. They go on the principle that the day begins at night."

These keen observations made by Ceasar make his accounts reliable to historians. Caesar also informs us that though there were no Druids in ancient Germany, they believed in the powers of the sun, moon, fire and other nature Gods, which the Vedic people worshipped. These aspects helped Indologists and perhaps Talageri claim that the ancestors of the Druids were none other than people of the Druhyu tribe who migrated out of India. However, many controversies are attached to this theory, like any pre-historical aspects.

Other Tribes Defeated in the Dasarajna War

The Prathu or Parthavas mentioned in the RV (7.83.1) were Parthians who made big later in the northeastern parts of Iran and the adjoining Central Asian region. Parsus or Parsavas (7.83.1) were Persians. Pakthas (7.18.7) and Bhalanas were Pakhtuns and Baluchis of Afghanistan. So far, so good. But in the case of all other tribes referred to in the RV, the controversies galore.

The Sivas (7.18.7) and Visanins are yet to be identified with the people of the present era. But Talageri identifies them as Khivas (from Uzbekistan) and Pishachas or Dards (people from East Afghanistan and Kashmir). He also identifies Bhrigus (the RV (7.18.6)— went along with the Anus) as Phrygians (people from Old Anatolia). He also informs us that the Simyus (RV 7.18.5) are Sarmatians (from the Ural Mountains, later settled in southern Russia). The Alinas (the RV 7.18.7) are Alans who were ancient Iranian pastoral nomadic people. But these contentions are subject to scrutiny as the final verdict has not yet come.

Similarly, most debates are reserved for the Anus of the Rigveda. Talageri categorically tells us that they are the ancestors of present-day Iranians. However, some people argue that 'Anu' is 'not a tribe' but is the 'King of Druhyus's name.'

Let us leave the controversies to the academicians.

There is a mention of more than fifty tribes in the Rigveda. It is not easy to name the descendants of each of those. But from the above discussions, it becomes clear that if many new tribes entered the Indian subcontinent, it is also true that an equal number of tribes from the Indian side went westwards in search of greener pastures—and they succeeded. Thus, no populace in the world can claim that they are the original inhabitants of a particular area from time immemorial. Such credit can only be reserved for Africans who still live in the deepest part of central Africa, where civilisation is yet to reach. We can give the same credit to a few surviving people of the Jarawa tribe of the Nicobar Islands.

Did the Steppe people come in or not?

Nobody can claim that foreign people have not entered the Indian subcontinent. They did trickle in, for sure. But they were in no position to influence the cultural milieu of the subcontinent as they came in as ravished immigrants shunted out from their homelands. Similarly, the people from the subcontinent moved to West Asia and Central Asia assimilated into other civilisations. The same has happened to the people who came to India through these Western frontiers.

The Steppe people came in and assimilated, at best, into the Vedic culture. These people were not in a position to dominate the Aryans. The Aryans were none other than the people of the Sarasvati basin who composed the Rigveda for hundreds of years before vacating the river basin because of the disappearance of the once-mighty river system.

Few bands of immigrants from abroad could have taken hundreds of years before affecting the local populace culturally or otherwise. If these foreign invaders were to be the authors of the sacred scripture, they would have recorded the names of their homelands and conquests in the text. The text talks only about the Indian subcontinent and its topography—not a single word about their earlier habitat. Suppose these invaders were to enter India around fifteen hundred BCE. They might have seen only a tiny rivulet instead of a mighty Sarasvati. If they composed the scriptures, they would not eulogise the river Sarasvati. We must also remember that they crossed mighty rivers, such as the Sindhu on their way into the Indian central land through the western frontiers. Despite all these crushing shreds of evidence, it is still fashionable for many to accept the trite Western theories.

✳✳✳

Conclusions

Western philosophers, historians, scientists and intellectuals have praised the Vedas for different reasons. If a few are impressed by Sanskrit's richness and rustic beauty, some are amazed by its magical construct. In comparison, philosophers wondered why other religions could not think about the sublime life lessons they contained. Scientists, including Einstein, were bewildered by the audacity of the text about the alternative stories of creation that it had. The intellectuals are impressed by the honesty of the epic in admitting what is not known.

But what astonishes everybody is the evolution of various Gods, methods of worship and later, the transformation to pure philosophical aspects. 'One Book' people (Western Monotheists) would not have allowed the changes as it would be considered blasphemous to question the contents of the book. But the Vedas accommodate different ideas without any fuss and ultimately, declare that "Ekam Sat, Viprah Bahuda Vadanti" (wise men give different names to the Ultimate Truth)and state that the ultimate goal in life must be to realise that Ultimate Reality, which is present in all the beings. The Vedic religion is the only one to support one God and many Gods simultaneously, which is unparalleled in the history of world religions.

If you look at what the RV propagates at the beginning of its older Mandalas (or Chapters) is the worship of the all-powerful Indra. The Rigveda also eulogises the other companion gods like Fire, Sun, Moon, the Maruts (storm Gods), Apa (Water), Prithvi and Akasha. Eventually, the RV dumps them subtly in the later Mandalas. When you come to the last and most recent chapter (The Tenth Mandala), you will see completely different and exhilarating ideas about the world order. While compiling it, its editor, Shakala includes all its old verses with their glory. He could have easily skipped all those ancient mantras and incorporated only the newer ideas. Yet, it would have been an excellent read. Shakala and his companion rishis did not take the easier route to concise the edition. Instead, they compiled all the mantras, including the old ones. The text has become a testimony to the all-inclusive ideas of an emerging religion which evolved tremendously over time. From that perspective, the RV is unique and secular.

The RV is candid and forthright in its approach and does not hide anything from us. It talks freely about habits, lifestyles, likes and dislikes, love and sex without any inhibition. We need not have to be embarrassed about its contents. On the other hand, we must be proud of our legacy.

What Will Durant Said About Our Past

In one of his articles, the most respected historian of the US, Will Durant, wrote, "India was the motherland of our race and Sanskrit is the mother of Europe's languages. She was the mother of our philosophy—mother through the Arabs, of much of our mathematics, mother through the Buddha of the ideals embodied in Christianity, mother through the village community of self-government and democracy. Mother India is, in many ways, the mother of us all."

Many Westerners concede significant contributions from India to the emergence of civilisation in the known world. Greece has been seen as the birthplace of art, philosophy, democracy and other finer aspects of civilised life in the West. Plato and Aristotle and their writings influenced people extensively—even the Christian world. Of course, both of them, in turn, were disciples of Socrates.

However, in the pre-Socratarian era, Pythagoras (Yes, whose famous mathematical theorem we mugged up in our middle school) was the name to reckon with—as a philosopher of repute, who hailed from Ionian Greece. At the end of his life, he was said to have led an ascetic's life with his community of followers in Croton, South Italy. He believed in the soul's immortality and preached that the soul migrated to another body after death. He enforced a strict vegetarian diet on all the commune members who meditated and participated in debates as ancient rishis would. Aristotle, in one of his writings, makes Pythagoras's double say the following:

"Humans exist to observe heaven. I keep observing nature and that is the reason why I came to life."

For ancient Indians, nature worship was common, but maybe it was a rebellion for the Greeks of that era. The Pythagorean community faced persecution for their novel ideas of religion.

In one of his talks, Professor Micheal Danino lists similarities between the religious beliefs of India and Greece of that epoch. In the Vedic era, we had Indra, Varuna, Usha, Surya, Durga and Bhu. The Greeks worshipped Zeus, Quranos, Aurora, Helios, Athena and Gaia. For our Devas and Asuras, they had Gods and Titans. The Vedic Gods drank Amrita, and Greeks called it Ambrosia. Pythagoreans and Plato believed in rebirth, and so did ancient Indians. Pythagoreans showed respect for all life forms, and so did Indians. Brahma's Egg was the World Egg for the Greeks.

Now, look at what Plato tells us about people and how he categorises them. He contends that all citizens are born out of the earth. Each soul is mixed with a specific metal at the time of creation. He tells us that the souls mixed with gold are suitable to rule. Silver is integrated into the souls of 'Auxiliaries' (soldiers) and Bronze or Iron is in the souls of producers or other craftsmen. Instead of calling them Brahmanas, Kshatriyas and Shudras, he categorises them as the gold, silver and iron classes. Accordingly, the roles are assigned, and he warned that if the lower class tries to rule, the country is bound to perish. It is up to you to decide whether it is the same as the Rigvedic classification. The pantheon of Gods is similar and the other resemblances are striking. The Rigveda is much older than all the writings of the Greek Philosophers.

Finally, the Pythagoras theorem has roots in Shulba Sutras by Rishi Baudhayana of the Vedic period. This theorem has been put on record by about four rishis, including Baudhayana, five hundred years before Pythagoras.

As a consolation, T. Lomperis, a research scholar, wrote thus, "Plato, through the Pythagoreans and the Orphics, was subjected to the influence of Hindu thought, but he may not have been aware of it as coming from India."

Here is a word of caution. It is not essential to know who copied whom, but knowing that the ancient world was better connected than we thought is heartening. The interaction and exchange of ideas in the ancient world were very robust. Rosaries, bells, incense, holy water, oil lamps, cave temples and 'chaityas' have reached other parts of the world. The Christians thought it was their invention and started using them for religious purposes.

"The similarities between the Gnostic Gospels, the Vedic teachings, and the Buddha's preachings must have compelled later Christians to dump the Gospels of Thomas, Philip, Judas, Mary and Truth," notes Micheal Danino.

In his book, 'Two Masters, One Message,' Roy Amore traces many parables and events in The New Testament to Buddhist stories. Roy even claims that The Sermon on the Mount has the highest concentration of the Buddhist saying. We know that the Buddha had first-hand knowledge of the Vedic religion of India. He studied the Vedas intensely before establishing a new religion.

The Rigveda vs. The Psalms

According to Britannica, The Psalms (or the Psalter) are books of The Old Testament composed of sacred songs or poems meant to be sung. In The Hebrew Bible, The Psalms begin the third and last section of the Biblical canon. In its present form, The Book of Psalms consists of one hundred and fifty poems. It is divided into five chapters. The poems exhibit a range of moods and expressions of faith, from joyous celebration to solemn hymns and bitter protest.

The Psalms had a profound effect on the development of Christian worship. Luke believed The Psalms to be a source of guidance. At the same time, Paul called on the faithful to sing psalms, hymns and spiritual songs. The early Church chanted these poems as part of the liturgy. There are four types of Psalms.

The Psalms of Confidence describes trust and faith in God. Let us examine some of the chants:

* "I will exalt you, Lord, for you lifted me out of the depths and did not let my enemies gloat over me." (The Psalms 30.1)

* "Lord, my God, I called to you for help, and you healed me." (The Psalms 30.2)

* "What is gained if I am silenced—if I go down to the pit? Will the dust praise you? Will it proclaim your faithfulness?" (30.9)

✱ "That my heart may sing your praises and not be silent. Lord my God, I will praise you forever." (30.12)

To quote the Bible Group, "The Psalms are impassioned, vivid and concrete. They are rich in images, similes and metaphors. Assonance, alliteration and wordplays abound in the Hebrew text. Effective repetition and the piling up of synonyms and complements to fill out the picture are characteristic. Keywords frequently highlight major themes in prayer or song…"

The Psalms or The Psalters make its debut at the temple built by the mythological king of combined Israel, David, in Jerusalem after its conquest. Interestingly, half of the chants tell the story of King David. We know the famous fight between him and the mighty Goliath, which he wins with a well-aimed slingshot. King David charmed people with his songs and his soothing harp music. Despite David's adultery and other sins, his people worshipped him.

King David is like the Rigvedic hero, Indra, for the people of Israel. When I went through many Psalms in addition to the ones mentioned above, I could see an apparent influence of Rigvedic verses on the spirit of the poems. The structure of the poetry used in The Psalms undoubtedly matches the Rigveda. Thus, it is fair to assume that the Rigveda has left its mark on all the religions of monotheism.

The Gist of the Evolution of Indian Religious Thoughts

We moved on to Upanishadic values from worshipping the great god, Indra and his companions in the Vedic epoch. Self-exploration gained prominence. The Upanishads grandly declared, "Abandon the search for God. Look for him by taking yourself as the starting point. Understand and look for the Ultimate Reality, which is within you. If you meditate upon your body, mind, soul and thought and carefully investigate these matters, you will find 'Moksha.'

But the 'Moksha' was to be attained after one's death.

However, the Buddha was looking for salvation during this birth only. Therefore on attaining enlightenment, he pronounced, touching the earth with his finger, "You can achieve salvation (Nirvana) here and now if you conquer four causes for your sufferings."

A subtle and sophisticated change to the Indian philosophy made him an instant celebrity and his followers surged in numbers.

Some scholars taunted Acharya Shankara as 'Prachanna' (disguised) Buddha during his lifetime. However, what he said had electrified and rejuvenated the sagging morale of the Vedic religion in the eighth century. He thundered in his inimitable style, "Aham Brahmasmi" (I am the God or the Ultimate Truth). This Maha Vakya or great saying comes from Brihadaranyaka Upanishad. Shankara quoted and emphasized strongly on its importance for individual salvation. He was suggesting but not saying openly that you can attain 'Moksha' through self-realisation in this world itself.

The World Is One Family

We know whoever entered India in the last two thousand and five hundred years as invaders or otherwise had forgotten their roots. It is evident from the known history that they did not keep their original language. "Where is the question of imposing their language on the natives?" asks Koenraad Elst.

It is unlikely that multiple bands of people from the Yamnaya region could impose their language and culture on the superior people of the Indus Valley area. On the contrary, the reverse must have happened. The intruders must have adopted the language and culture of native Indians and become part of the Vedic society.

But the truth is that the world and its populace benefitted from the barter system. Barter of genes, goods and services, knowledge, technology, ideas, religious thoughts, etc., benefited generations throughout the aeons, and helped us reach thus far as a civilisation.

Whenever some new evidence emerged from the Harappan excavations, the Aryan Invasion Theorists' voices weakened to that extent. After learning about the Indus Valley people, they could not call native Indians primitive and ill-informed. Hence, Michael Witzel used the text of the Rigveda to strengthen his theory. The new field of study, Genetics, has given him much support. Using this opportunity, Tony Joseph wanted to settle the

Aryan migration debate. Not to be outdone, Shrikant Talageri writes a solid rebuttal to both of them by arguing that the motherland of the Indo-European language was India. But, we must understand that Genetics, Language, Culture and Archaeology are double-edged swords. Each side can twist the theories to propagate their side of the story.

In the compendium of the Rigveda, we have a solid opportunity to clear the air on many contentious historical aspects. But, we must blame our ancestors for losing a more versatile and elaborate addition to the RV. The Bhashkala Samhita of the text would have been an immense help to historians if it had been available to us. Our scholars claim that we have thousands of manuscripts buried in private collections, in the temples' underground treasures that are yet to be dusted and read. Let us hope that one fine day, the lost edition surfaces to throw more light on the pre-historic period of India.

Alternatively, our Vedic pandits must shed their inhibitions and read the Rigveda afresh with an open mind to pick up historical inputs hidden in the text. Our libraries are already brimming with many philosophical thoughts emanating from the epic. The time has come for studying the scripture for equally crucial historical details to settle the Aryan issue. Let me end the discussions with a profound thought from the greatest scientist of the twentieth century:

"The important thing is to not stop questioning. Curiosity has its reason for existence. One cannot help but be in awe when they contemplate the mysteries of eternity of life, of the marvellous structure of reality. **It is enough if one tries merely to comprehend a little of this mystery each day.**"

– Albert Einstein.

***